Reading Stories with Young Children

Reading Stories with Young Children

Robin Campbell

Trentham Books

Stoke on Trent, UK and Sterling, USA

Trentham Books Limited
Westview House   22883 Quicksilver Drive
734 London Road   Sterling
Oakhill   VA 20166-2012
Stoke on Trent   USA
Staffordshire
England ST4 5NP

First published 2009

British Library Cataloguing-in-Publication Data
A catalogue record for this book is available from the British
Library

ISBN: 978 1 85856 452 4

Designed and typeset by Trentham Print Design Ltd, Chester
and printed in Great Britain by Page Bros (Norwich) Ltd.

Contents

1

Introduction

When young children have stories read to them as part of a normal day they learn about reading, they act like readers and they become readers with an interest in books. Young children demonstrate this to adults constantly. Recently, after just a couple of readings by an adult of *Four Fierce Kittens* (Dunbar, 1991), Louie age 3 years, 9 months demonstrated how much he had learned of a repeated sentence in the story:

Adult   *Said the marmalade kitten,*
spiking her claws
'I am a terrible tiger!
I shall hunt hen out of her hutch.'
And she tried to growl

Louie   *(But she didn't know how)*
She could only go...
miaow miaow
And hen went
CLUCK CLUCK CLUCK

Adult   *Said the black little kitten*
with a glint in his eye ...

Louie acted like a reader as he recalled a repeated sentence of the story. So although he was not yet attending directly to the print, he was well on the way to becoming a reader.

Reading stories with young children at home and in school has a long and illustrious history. Huey (1908) argued that the parent and the young child reading a book was the road to success: 'the secret of it all lies in parent's reading aloud to and with the child' (p332). A century later an overview of the research on reading aloud led by Zuckerman concluded that reading stories at home 'promotes emergent literacy and language development' and 'a love of reading' (Duursma, Augustyn and Zuckerman, 2008). There are numerous studies that have emphasised the importance of reading stories with young children. When we create book-loving schools and homes children respond by wanting to read (Michael Rosen.co.uk). The enjoyment, the learning and the encouragement of the child towards reading have all sustained the activity.

But recently the primary school curriculum has become saturated with documents, strategies, targets and testing, testing, testing. So much so that sometimes there may appear to be so many accountability boxes to be ticked and plans to complete that fundamental aspects of literacy can be forgotten. Sadly, story reading is one key area that might seem possible to put to one side, as other more mundane activities have to be shown to be completed. Yet story reading must remain as a daily feature of primary school life because the literacy learning thus achieved and the desire to read that is created are far too important to be lost.

An earlier book of mine appeared in the USA with the title *Read-Alouds with Young Children* (Campbell, 2001). The term 'read-aloud' is used in the United States to describe the worldwide phenomenon of an adult reading a book to and with a young child or a group of children (Trelease, 1995). Another text from America, although written by Australian author Mem Fox (2001), refers to 'Reading Aloud to Our Children'. In New Zealand the same practice

2

is termed 'storybook reading' (Phillips and McNaughton, 1990) while in the United Kingdom it is most often called 'story reading' (Campbell, 1990) or simply *Reading stories with young children.*

This book explores reading stories both at home and at school with young children. Most of the observations for it took place in classrooms in England, predominately nursery or pre-school classrooms with 3 and 4 year olds, 5 year olds in reception class and 6 and 7 year olds in years 1 and 2. A few observations extended to other primary classrooms up to year 6 (age 11).

A story reading can stand alone as an enjoyable activity, but for most children being able to respond to the story extends their enjoyment and furthers their understanding. *Reading stories with young children* focuses on the reading and the activities that can be developed from it. Teachers of young children and teacher educators may find this book useful as a means of reconsidering story reading and its contribution to a literacy curriculum. Parents too will be interested to note how reading stories at home provides a foundation for children's reading and writing development.

During readings the adult often encourages the youngest children to participate as the story is being read. So Louie was already contributing key phrases during a story reading when he was 2 years old.

Adult   *'A leak in the roof.*
         Oh, what bad luck!
         This is a job for...'

Louie   *'Fix-It Duck.'*

In that instance the frequent use at the end of a sentence of *Fix-It Duck* (Alborough, 2001) made it easy for Louie to become part of the interactive reading. In other books the use of rhyming like *luck/duck* helps the child to contribute to the reading.

Then subsequently, not only do the children contribute, they also respond in various ways to the story that has been read (Neuman,

3

1998). The interactive story reading is an important literacy acti-vity that is recognised as a developmentally appropriate practice for young children (International Reading Association, 1998). Sup-port for the activity includes research evidence from projects ex-ploring literacy development at home, and explorations of story readings in schools. The power of the interactive story readings to support children's literacy learning is enhanced when those read-ings are repeated (McGee and Schickedanz, 2007).

Literacy development at home

The Children Learning to Read Project, the longitudinal study directed by Gordon Wells in Bristol, is frequently cited. In this study, children were observed from shortly after their first birthday until they were 10 years old. It was found that the children who demonstrated a relatively high understanding of print as they started school at age 5 were more likely to achieve high levels of reading at age 10. But how was that understanding of print ac-quired? The researchers found that the parents' story readings had a positive influence on the literacy development of their children and that listening to stories significantly related to the children's understanding of print (Wells, 1986). In addition, the opportuni-ties for children to watch their parents handle the books and to be involved in discussions about the story were all valuable aspects of the story reading.

Shirley Brice Heath (1983) confirmed the value of parents reading stories for pre-school children and the importance of the inter-active experience. She studied the literacy experiences of pre-school children in three neighbouring communities in the United States. The communities each demonstrated different adult prac-tices, and these led to different outcomes for the children at school. In one community, the parents read storybooks interactively to their children. As we would expect, the children in that environ-ment were successful at reading in school. In another community, the parents read to their children and helped them with letter names, but did not encourage the children to be involved in the story readings – the readings were not interactive. The children did well at school initially and managed tasks such as completing workbook pages, but they were less successful in the later elementary grades. The children in the third community were the least successful at reading in school. Although the parents valued school for the benefits it might afford their children, they did not provide the same learning environment at home and seldom read stories to their children.

Denny Taylor and Dorothy Strickland (1986) also discuss the benefits of family storybook readings, but take a different approach. They provide numerous excerpts from parent-child read-alouds, and there are many illustrations that demonstrate the intensity of the children's involvement. The read-alouds from many different homes demonstrate the learning that takes place beyond the story itself. The authors show how the children learned a sense of how stories are constructed, and how that helped them understand many other stories and create their own. The children also extended their vocabulary as they interacted with their parents during the story readings. They learned not only individual words but the language patterns contained in stories, and they began to play with the sounds of language. The story reading experience also reinforced the listening skills the children later used to support their classroom learning.

Although Taylor and Strickland's book focuses on storybook readings, it also links with a main theme of *Reading stories with young children*: the readings can provide the basis for other activities. Their findings show that stories that are read aloud inspire children and parents to create their own books. So the authors suggest that the children should have a thick pad of plain paper and a box of crayons or felt pens to make their own response to the stories. These responses can lead to parents and children working together to make their own family storybooks. In one example they report on a child who extends her interest in cats to create her own storybook about them; this exemplifies how children use their experiences to draw and write with feeling (pp75-76). Reading stories with young children works. Mem Fox (2001) argues passionately that being read to at home in enjoyable interactions, enables children to become readers. And reporting on the Bookstart project, Wade and Moore (2000) and Collins and Svensson (2008) noted that young children who share books with an adult at home achieve well when they go to school. They do so because they learn from books, they learn about books and they learn literacy.

Children developing as literacy users

A number of longitudinal studies of individual children add to our understanding of the importance of reading stories to young children. These studies typically follow children in their first five years of life. In many cases the researchers were studying their own children, but because these studies are numerous, we can look objectively at the data they provide. One of the best known studies is that of Glenda Bissex (1980). Bissex read stories to her son Paul before he started to talk; these readings supported Paul to recognise stories and provide an emergent reading before he turned 3.

Judith Schickedanz (1990) reports on the development of her son Adam's writing, indicating that Adam sought repeated readings of favourite books from about 16 months until the age of 3 years. After that his preference was for information-rich non-fiction books. In other studies by parents and grandparents of young children (Baghban, 1984; Laminack, 1991; Martens, 1996; Whitehead, 2002) there is evidence to suggest that story readings are an important contributor to a child's literacy development. Baghban includes transcripts to show how her daughter Giti developed as a reader from the age of 30 to 33 months as she returned frequently to reread texts she already knew.

A few studies have concentrated more exclusively on the interactions between parents and children during read-alouds. Jones

(1996) was unusual in that she limited her study to the first two years of their lives. She noted the physical, mental, and emotional pleasures of the readings. Spreadbury (1994) and Doake (1988) followed children for a longer period of time, and both indicated that story readings were important in supporting literacy development. Doake concluded that 'children who are read to regularly by their parents and teachers are being given what they are entitled to in a society that expects them to become fully literate' (p48).

In addition, there are two studies (Campbell, 1999; White, 1954/ 1984) that specifically record a child's development in conjunction with read-alouds. Dorothy White, a librarian, shared a wide variety of books with her daughter Carol between the ages of 2 and 5. White's study presents a diary of those shared readings and demonstrates the enormous enjoyment that came from the readings and the influence of the books on Carol's language and play. In *Literacy from home to school: reading with Alice* (Campbell, 1999), I report on how my granddaughter Alice listened to stories read to her daily, including many repeated readings of favourite books. My study includes transcripts of Alice's involvement in the story readings and shows her progress as a reader from birth to 5 years of age. She started to make a verbal contribution to the reading of a short book when she was almost 2. Then she extended those contributions with other books until she memorised whole stories. That memorisation enabled her to begin to see links with the print, and at 3 years 9 months, she made known that attention to print when sharing *Zoo Animals* (Butterfield, 1995):

Alice: Look there's *and* and *zoo*.

Grandfather: Yes, that says *and* and that word is *zoo*. It's a book about zoo animals, isn't it?

Alice: Mmh, I like the hippo best.

Grandfather: That hippo gets all muddy, doesn't it?

(Campbell, 1999, p86)

Alice's recognition of some print enabled her to begin to read from previously shared books. All these events contributed to her willingness to read short unfamiliar books by the time she was 5 years old. Reading stories with adults, some of them many times over, was key to supporting that development. And Whitehead (2002) used her observations of her grandson Dylan during his first three years of engagement with picture books to demonstrate that boys too enjoy and learn from storybooks. Nevertheless in primary classrooms, it can be important for teachers to ensure that plenty of the books read to the children provide role models for the boys (Zambo, 2007).

Reading stories in school

Do story readings work in a similarly effective way in school? The study of story readings in school by Feitelson, Kita, and Goldstein (1986) is frequently cited. The authors followed two teachers who were working with first-grade classes as they read to the children for 20 minutes at the end of the school day. One of the teachers believed that the reading consumed too much time, so she stopped the daily readings. When given reading tests at the end of the study, the children in the class that continued with read-alouds performed measurably better.

Smith and Elley (1994) briefly review the outcomes of some of the research dealing with story readings, including some earlier work by Elley (1989) that demonstrates vocabulary gains among 8 and 9 year-old children from stories that were read to them. They did better still when the teacher explained or illustrated the target words. Morrow (1992) notes literacy gains among children from minority backgrounds when a literature-based program was developed with second year children in the USA. An important part of the programme was the daily reading of stories and the activities developed from them.

Learning from story readings

It is difficult to isolate the literacy gains that accrue from story readings, but the activity does appear to provide many benefits for young children. Marriott (1995) asserts boldly that 'it is almost impossible to overemphasise the value of this activity for children of any age or reading level' (p65).

Story readings provide the basis for children to learn about literacy, to become readers and writers, to learn through literacy and to want to read in the future (Sloan, 1991). At the same time, we are reminded by writers such as Money (1987) that teachers should ensure that the child's response to and enjoyment of the story or poem remains paramount.

Children arrive at pre-school or primary school with a wide range of differing experiences of books. Some have had the joy of hearing hundreds of stories read to and with them. And because a story is often read aloud more than once, these children may have experienced thousands of story readings. If the teacher continues with readings and repeat readings of a story, it gives the children a link between home and school. They can extend and develop their literacy learning at once because they are in the familiar territory of narrative, with its interesting characters, stimulating events and thought-provoking outcomes.

Children who have not been read to at home, benefit from having frequent and regular story readings in their classroom. They need to explore the delights of storybooks supported by adults who read to them and discuss aspects of the stories. As Moustafa (1997) maintained:

> The primary literacy education task of pre-school and early school years is not teaching children letter-sound correspondences but reading to them. Reading to children in school should be a daily activity, as important a part of a child's class schedule as math and lunch. If a child is experiencing difficulty in learning to read, we should not ask if he or she knows the sounds of letters but if he or she has been read to extensively. (p78-79)

This affirms Well's view (1986). He notes in his case study of Rosie, a child who apparently had never been read to before starting school, that she needed a personal introduction to literacy through stories (p159). One-on-one story readings actively involve children in the reading. Many teachers, especially when they have adult helpers in the classroom, can provide one-to-one story readings on a regular basis in addition to class readings. Frequently, during these one-to-one readings, other children will place themselves close enough to listen in; such is the power and enjoyment of stories.

How does literacy develop through reading stories? First, children learn about literacy because they have an adult providing a model of reading. The story reading provides an understanding at a simple level of how print functions and how it is used (Strickland and Morrow, 1989). As children watch adults use books to read aloud, they quickly become aware of and knowledgeable about left-to-right and front-to-back directionality. In the classroom Holdaway (1979) suggests that the teacher might use Big Books for some story readings so all the children can see the print and follow that process of reading.

But children learn far more from story readings than how to use a book (Butler, 1998). Children learn about the structure of stories – the beginning, the middle, and the end. Furthermore, as Dombey (1988) indicates, children learn new words, new sentences and new discourse patterns. When the children have the opportunity to explore in writing the stories that have been read aloud with them, that learning is extended. Fox (1993) indicates how literature influences children's own storytelling. Her record of young children's storytelling demonstrates how the stories children have heard feed into their own stories.

Children also develop knowledge and understanding of letters and letter-sound relationships (Campbell, 2004). Moustafa (1997) argues that the starting point for young children is hearing stories rather than learning letters, but the children do nevertheless learn about letters from stories. For example, it is not hard to imagine the learning about letters and sounds that might follow rereadings of Sniff-Snuff-Snap! (Dodd, 1995), in which the consonant blend sn is so prominent. This learning would occur even when the emphasis is on the enjoyment of this delightful story.

In Teale's (1984) analysis of the benefits that accrue from stories read aloud, he includes the development of positive attitudes toward reading. In part, these attitudes originate from the shared enjoyment of the story. But they also come from the way in which stories can provide tales about lives and events outside the child's own experience (Trelease, 1995). Story readings can encourage children's positive attitudes toward books because they offer the chance to learn about a wider world.

Organisation of this book

In order to look more closely at story readings, Chapter 2 explores the activity in a reception classroom. It is not always possible to watch, or listen to, a reading of a story in a classroom, but this chapter enables us to enter the classroom and observe what takes place. It includes transcript excerpts from the teacher reading the story and the children's comments and questions. We also see how a number of activities develop from this lively, enjoyable reading.

Preparing for a story reading is examined in Chapter 3. A successful story reading will depend on several things: selecting an appropriate book to read, preparing carefully for the story reading, performing the reading enthusiastically and ensuring that the children take part.

Chapter 4 considers the importance of narrative as a way of thinking. It suggests that reading stories encourages children to think in a particular way so as to construct a sense of reality. Story also enhances children's literacy skills, supports their cultural heritage and aids their personal development. To achieve these benefits, children must be exposed to books of quality. The chapter explores the use of predictable storybooks with repetition, rhyme and rhythm and highlights the importance of poetry and non-fiction texts.

Chapter 5 notes how the story reading can support detailed learning about letter and word print features such as the alphabet, phonics and spelling. The children's involvement with stories and the writing that follows creates numerous opportunities to think about graphophonic connections. The stories also provide a starting point for the teacher to create a word wall that aids the children's learning.

The children's interest in the story reading frequently leads them into other activities that link to the story. Chapter 6 discusses how role playing, drawing and writing, making books, creating arts and crafts, making and using puppets and singing songs and rhymes can all be part of the children's response. Sometimes it is the teacher who encourages the children in that direction; on other occasions it is the children who immediately want to follow the reading in a particular way.

When the teacher reads a story from a Big Book, the activity is transformed. All the children can see the print, so the teacher can emphasise print features. Shared reading with Big Books is the subject of Chapter 7, along with sustained silent reading, individual reading, buddy reading, paired reading, guided reading and literature circles.

Similarly the stories, poems and rhymes that have been read aloud are a good starting point for shared writing. Chapter 8 considers how the teacher demonstrates writing and the discussions that take place during this activity. Other linked activities such as interactive writing, guided writing and individual writing are explored.

The stories that are read aloud create opportunities for many different activities to take place. They also lead into other curriculum areas such as mathematics, science and social studies. Often the children inquire about the facts that are contained within the stories. At other times the teacher plans to use the story as a starting point for a study in another curriculum area. Chapter 9 examines how stories can provide the stimulus for exploring a variety of issues.

The short concluding chapter reminds us that a great deal of learning flows from stories that are read aloud. Teachers should ensure that a variety of possibilities exist for children to follow a well-read story and to find enjoyment in the process.

The opportunities for developing the curriculum from story readings are endless. At the same time, teachers should remember that the main objective is to provide interesting books for the children, that will engage their thinking and emotions. The activities that are developed from the story must not dampen the children's enthusiasm for stories and reading. And no story should be overused to the point that children lose their enthusiasm for it. In Powell and Hornsby's (1998) words:

> Since all text is language, all texts have numerous possibilities for highlighting different aspects of language. There is no need to milk a book dry of skills and bore your students in the process; it is better to use the skills possibilities available in a variety of literature and other authentic texts. (p84)

The secret of success with reading stories rests with the sensitivity of the adult at home and, subsequently, the professional approach of the teacher. With the right balance, reading stories can help children improve their learning skills and develop a love of reading that will last a lifetime. The following chapters illustrate how this works.

2

Reading stories interactively

In a reception classroom

Another busy day in a classroom of 30 5-year-old children in London was drawing to a close. The teacher gathered the children around her and prepared to read a story.

Teacher:	What do you think this book is about?
Ben:	A caterpillar.
David:	It's got lots of hairs.
Matthew:	And green eyes.
Sophie:	Why is it wearing shoes?
Teacher:	They do look like shoes, but they are the caterpillar's feet. It's a story about a very hungry caterpillar, and the author is Eric Carle.
Ben:	Yeah, those letters tell us.

The Very Hungry Caterpillar (Carle, 1969) has been and continues to be enjoyed by millions of children across the world. The appealing nature of the main character, the rhythm and repetition of the text and the trail of holes left by the caterpillar through the pages all add to the attraction.

Before the teacher began reading to the 5-year-olds, she intro-duced the book. She encouraged the children to make comments about the front cover and the caterpillar. She told them the author's name. One child indicated where the teacher got this information from. The reading was already demonstrating what Strickland and Morrow (1989) describe as a 'co-operative con-struction of meaning between the adult and child' (p323). The literacy event was interactive, and the children were encouraged to contribute comments and questions.

The children's involvement was maintained as the teacher started to read the first page:

Amy: I can see the moon.

Denise: It's smiling.

Teacher: It does look like it's smiling.

                In the light of the moon
                a little egg lay on a leaf.

Sally: I can see it; it's white.

Teacher: It is, isn't it?

When the teacher reached the pages where the caterpillar eats a different fruit on each day from Monday to Friday, there was great excitement:

Danny: There are lots of holes in the book.

John: And fruit.

Teacher: Yes, there are different fruits with holes. I wonder why there are holes in the fruit?

Ben: That's where the caterpillar eats.

John: He nibbles holes.

Matthew: I like fruit.

Stephanie:	So do I.
Teresa:	I like strawberries.
Teacher:	Yes, I thought you would, and so did the very hungry caterpillar.

> *On Monday*
> *he ate through*
> *one apple.*
> *But he was still*
> *hungry.*

The holes in the book intrigue children. The five different fruits also elicit comments, as we see when the teacher encouraged the children to take part in the story reading by accepting and responding to their observations. The teacher used their comments to lead back into the reading of the story in a natural manner. Her actions contributed to the children's literacy learning and were an important part of the management of the class.

As the teacher continued with the story, the children extracted fine detail from the illustrations. For example, when they reached Thursday, one child commented on the strawberries:

Jamie:	Four strawberries-one's upside down.
Teacher:	There are four strawberries.

> *On Thursday*
> *he ate through*
> *four strawberries*

When a child makes a remark of this nature, it encourages others in the class to look carefully at the pictures and eventually at the print. (Newer editions of this book have each of the strawberries in a vertical position!)

The children also made links from the story to their own feelings. As the teacher repeated the refrain, Ben expressed his own hunger.

Teacher:	*but he was still*
	hungry.
Ben:	I'm hungry. Is it home time?
Teacher:	Nearly; you'll soon be able to have a snack.

The two-page spread in the book for Saturday would add to Ben's hunger, and other children also commented on the illustration of the food the caterpillar consumed on Saturday:

John:	Look at all that food.
Danny:	There's a lollipop. I like lollipops.

The teacher responded by reading the corresponding text and asked why the caterpillar ended up with a stomach-ache.

Ben:	He had too much food.
Jamie:	I like all that food
Amy:	He was greedy.
Teacher:	That's right; he ate too much. But what else gave it a stomach-ache?
Sophie:	Real caterpillars eat leaves.
Teacher:	Yes, they do, Sophie. The caterpillar ate the wrong food and it gave him a stomach-ache.
Joanne:	He needs medicine.
Ben:	My mum gives me stuff when I'm not well.
Teacher:	Yes, you have some medicine. Well...
	The next day was Sunday again.
	The caterpillar ate through
	one nice green leaf
Sophie:	Now he'll be better.
Teacher:	Yes.

> *and after that he felt*
> *much better.*

Clearly the children remained very involved with the story. They related it to events in their own lives. The interaction between the teacher and the children took more time than the actual reading of the story. This is often the case, especially when a book is read aloud for the first time, and particularly in reception or pre-school classrooms.

As the story reaches its conclusion, the caterpillar builds a cocoon. This development intrigued the children.

Samuel: It looks like a stone.

Pavi: That's a funny house.

Teacher: Yes, it's a cocoon. And after he pushed his way out of the cocoon...

> *he was a beautiful butterfly!*

Danny: That's pretty.

Teresa: I saw a butterfly in my garden.

Teacher: So you saw a beautiful butterfly in your garden?

Teresa: Yes, but it wasn't all those colours. It was nearly all white.

Teacher: Was it? I wonder what it looked like when it was a caterpillar.

Other children wanted to talk about seeing white butterflies and green caterpillars. As they left the classroom, they were still talking about the story, caterpillars and butterflies, and food to be eaten. They had enjoyed the story. They contributed to the reading by asking questions, making comments and relating the story to their own experiences and they remained excited about the story.

This account demonstrates the benefits of reading stories and shows why teachers of young children use this literacy activity so often. Many teachers read a story at the beginning of the day so they can capitalise on the children's excitement by providing immediate opportunities for them to explore the story in various ways. In this example, the teacher chose to read the story at the end of the school day because she knew the children would talk about it at home and therefore develop their ideas about it before returning to school.

Repeat readings

The next morning, the teacher reminded the children of the story. The reading and the children's subsequent talk and thinking about the story provided a strong background for the events of the day:

Teacher: Do you remember *The Very Hungry Caterpillar*?

Jamie: I liked that story.

Ben: He eat [sic] all the wrong food.

Teacher: He did. He ate all the wrong food.

Michael: He's got a funny face.

Danny: Read it again.

Thus some of the children indicated their positive feelings toward the story and their recognition of a theme and they requested another reading. The teacher was expecting this response and had made preparations for another reading and for other activities linked to the story.

During the repeat reading, the interactions expanded. The rhythm and repetition that are part of this story encouraged the children to take part in the reading. The teacher began the refrain and paused, and this prompted the children to join in:

Teacher: *On Monday*
he ate through

	one apple.
	But [with emphasis and pausing for the children]
Children:	*he was still hungry.*
Matthew:	He eats lots of food.
Teacher:	He does. Now,

On Tuesday

By the time the teacher reached the Friday page, all the children were anticipating the refrain and joining in and doing so earlier, starting with *but*.

The children were also excited to give their opinions about the caterpillar and the foods that he ate on Saturday.

Danny:	He got a bellyache.
Anna:	He eats the wrong food.
Ben:	He eat [sic] people's food.
Amy:	He was greedy. (A repeat of her comment from the previous day, now given with some emphasis.)
Matthew:	He should have just eaten leaves.

Heath (1982, 1983) argues that as children participate in interactive story readings, they learn not only how to take meaning from books but how to talk about it. The children are able to provide 'what-explanations,' such as a description of what the topic is about. This provides the basis for children to provide explanations and affective commentaries. These may be requirements for the upper years of school as Heath suggests, but can also occur with younger children. In this example, Amy provided a reason why the caterpillar got stomach-ache, and Matthew suggested how the caterpillar could have avoided the problem. The interactive nature of the story reading supports and encourages such thinking.

21

The children remained very interested in the cocoon. They wanted to talk about the cocoon and to relate that to their own home and other types of houses.

Joanne:	He made a special house for himself.
Matthew:	Yeah, a cocoon.
Sally:	I live in a house.
Lewis:	I live in a flat.
Sophie:	My rabbit lives in a hutch.
Teacher:	Well done. People and animals live in different types of homes, and the caterpillar made his own house-a cocoon.

The teacher made it clear that she welcomed comments during the story reading, thus encouraging a pattern of interactive readings for the future. She confirmed the children's comments about the different types of houses that people and animals inhabit, and she reminded them that the caterpillar built his own house. She also repeated the name of that house: a cocoon.

This reading of a story gave the children the opportunity to behave like readers. And their memorisation of parts of the story helped them in the days and months ahead when they looked through the book on their own and started to read the print. In these ways, the story reading provided a foundation for literacy learning. After completing the story, the teacher asked the children what they liked about it. She prompted the class to reflect on the story and their feelings toward it. There were many responses:

Danny:	I liked it when he made holes in the fruit. He crawled in and out.
Ben:	I liked the bit where he eat [sic] all the wrong food and gave him a tummy-ache.
Joanne:	It tells us all about the butterfly.

These responses – along with the children's comments during the repeat reading, their contributions to the reading, and their excitement about the story at the start of the day – all suggest that they had benefited from the two readings. And that they would be interested in following the story with other activities.

Activities following the story reading

During the next few days, the children revisited and explored the story in a number of ways. The teacher suggested some of the activities and had already prepared materials for constructing puppets. Other ideas came from the children.

Stick puppets

The children made caterpillars out of dough, clay, cloth or cardboard. The teacher helped the children construct caterpillar stick puppets, which generated interest in creating stick puppets of other creatures or characters. She encouraged the children to use the puppets throughout the day as she reread parts of the story.

Children painted large pictures of chocolate cake, ice cream cones and the rest of the inappropriate food the caterpillar ate on Saturday. The teacher added large printed labels for each of these foods. Each time the teacher recited that part of the story and the children joined in, the children moved the puppets along the posters, crawling from one food to another.

What did this mean for the children's incidental learning? They memorised another part of the story, recalled the sequence of foods eaten on the Saturday, matched the book illustrations and student paintings to the story as it was recited, noted the teacher's large printed words under each picture, and worked collaboratively. Importantly they also had great fun.

Further readings

In addition to encouraging the children to use their puppets beside the posters, the teacher read the complete story many times because the children so enjoyed hearing it and often requested it. These further readings enabled the children to gain ownership of the story. They grew confident in their knowledge of it, became familiar with the main character, and could recall some of the key phrases for themselves. A few of them could recite much of the story on their own.

The frequent repeat readings of the book took place quite naturally within the classroom. As Teale and Sulzby (1989) argue, 'Repeated readings by the teacher are especially important' (p7). These replicate the valuable repeat readings that many children enjoy at home (Campbell, 1999) and encourage the children to read the book for themselves. Children enjoy having the stories repeated because it enables them to gain ownership of the words and meanings of the book. As Morrow (1988) notes, repeat readings lead the children to focus on print as well as story structure. As the children begin to memorise many of the book's words, they can recall some of the story when they look at each page. They can take part in the reading by offering some words, phrases and sentences as the adult reads aloud. In this way, they are able to behave like readers.

Singing rhymes

As we listen to young children engaged in various activities throughout the day, we can hear echoes of the story from the story reading. In this classroom the children often repeated key phrases such as 'but he was still hungry,' as they drew and painted. Their involvement with the story also extended into other linked rhymes, verses or songs.

To continue the shared book experience, the teacher used a song poster with large print as the basis for another literacy activity. As Holdaway (1979) notes, 'Some of [the] instructional reading material can be their songs – and poems' (p66). The teacher had prepared a poster with the words to a simple song that linked closely to *The Very Hungry Caterpillar*. In the song, the caterpillar is eating, and there is a sequence of eggs, caterpillar, pupa or cocoon, and butterfly – then back to eggs. The teacher followed the sequence with the children as she sang with them and pointed to the words on the poster:

> I went to the cabbages one day.
> What do you think I saw?
> Eggs in a cluster, yellow as a duster.
> What could it all be for?

> I went to the cabbages one day.
> What do you think I saw?
> Caterpillar crawling, caterpillar munching.
> What could it all be for?

> I went to the cabbages one day.
> What do you think I saw?
> I saw a super duper pupa.
> What could it all be for?

> I went to the cabbages one day.
> What do you think I saw?
> I saw a butterfly flutter by.
> What could it all be for?

> I went to the cabbages one day.
> What do you think I saw?
> Eggs in a cluster, yellow as a duster.
> What could it all be for?

As we expect from such events, the children soon picked up the words of the song. The first, second, and fourth lines are repeated in each verse, and the third line shows the life cycle of the butterfly, which the children had followed in Eric Carle's story. Within a few repeats of the song, the children were joining in confidently and enthusiastically. Songs such as this become a valuable resource for teachers, and a collection of verses and songs that complement story readings can be developed over time. The teacher also printed a short verse as a large poster. In this kindergarten class-room she used it with the children as a poem to be recited:

'Who's that tickling my back?'
said the wall.
'Me,' said a caterpillar,
'I'm learning to crawl.'

It became easy for the teacher to involve small groups of children to act out the words. With some children as the wall, others as the caterpillar, and groups to recite the verse, the children engaged again with the antics of a caterpillar. They also made connections between the words they recited and the print on the poster. By this time the printed word *caterpillar* had been seen, spoken and en-joyed in many different contexts. Many children were starting to recognise the word.

Drawing and writing

In addition to making the two posters, the teacher also created a small word wall. This ensured that some of the words from the story were readily available for the children in the classroom. The word wall was especially useful for the children who began to draw and write. Others needed to make less reference to the word wall because they were confident about taking risks with words; a risk taking that the teacher encouraged. These children produced their writing with their own invented spellings based on the sounds they heard in each word as they wrote.

Because of the nature of the story, many of the children produced drawings or collages of the caterpillar (see Figure 1). Additionally, some children included what the caterpillar ate. Others extended that line of thinking and drew pictures of different animals and what they liked to eat. Two of the children's drawings demonstrate this (see Figures 2 and 3).

Their writing also indicates their varying levels of understanding about print. In the example in Figure 2, the child produced four

Figure 1: Sample Caterpillar Collage

Figure 2: A Giraffe Eats Leaves

Figure 3: Crab Eats Fish

words: *A graff ates leves* (A giraffe eats leaves). One of the words is written conventionally, and the other three are close enough approximations to enable the reader to make sense of the child's effort. In particular, *graff* and *leves* demonstrate a good use of the graphophonic features and the child's growing knowledge of letters and sounds. Furthermore, each of the words appears within a space. The spacing can be contrasted with the example in Figure 3, where the writing of *CABET FS* (Crab eats fish) is more difficult to decipher, although the picture clue helps.

In Figure 3, the final word is separated from the other two, showing that the child, not quite 5 years old, had some knowledge of letters and sounds and was able to put that knowledge to good use while writing. Other children stayed more firmly with the story they had heard, writing it in their own words, often greatly abbreviated. For instance, as we see in Figure 4, Carly wrote only one sentence and she obviously used the word wall; each word is written conventionally.

Other children retold the story in their own words or wrote about some part of it. A few children let their imagination extend their view of the story. Richard linked the story to his other interests, writing about railways and roads (see Figure 5).

The teacher extended the link from the story reading to the children's writing by developing a class book. That book, titled *Our Caterpillar Stories* (see Figure 6), was placed in the classroom library alongside *The Very Hungry Caterpillar*. In each of these ways, the children remained involved with the story they had enjoyed.

Focus on the life cycle (science)

The Very Hungry Caterpillar is an ingenious book in several ways. In addition to providing a captivating story (Trelease, 1995), it teaches children about the days of the week and their sequence and it encourages them to think about the numbers 1 to 5. In addi-

Figure 4: Carly's Story

Figure 5: Richard's Story

Figure 6: Cover of Our Caterpillar Stories

Figure 7: Adrian's Picture

tion, it describes the life cycle of the butterfly, which the children learn from the frequent rereading.

The song also added to the children's scientific knowledge. As the song was sung in the classroom for the second time, one child remarked, 'This song can go on forever.' A few of the children, supported by the teacher, folded a sheet of paper into four sections and drew pictures of the cycle, showing eggs, caterpillar, cocoon, and butterfly. That led the children to re-create the science sequence and follow a simple story structure of beginning, middle and end.

Counting and measuring (mathematics)

Although the text encouraged the children to count from 1 to 5 with each of the weekday pages, the teacher used the children's interest in the main character to measure, compare, and count beyond 5. For instance, the children took great delight in drawing pictures of the caterpillars. They liked to follow the example set by Eric Carle and give them bold facial features. Adrian's picture of the caterpillar (see Figure 7) seemed to capture the main character particularly well.

As the children drew caterpillars, the class discussed their various lengths. Questions such as 'How long is your caterpillar?' and 'Who has got the longest caterpillar?' led the children to count with cubes and compare the lengths with others. Adam used his picture to measure the length of the caterpillar. He wrote that 'my caterpillar si [is] 14 squares long'. To make that calculation, he placed 14 maths cubes beside his picture and counted them. His coloured picture accurately reflects the number and colours of the 14 squares he used. Throughout this process, the children remained excited about their drawings and engaged incidentally in mathematical thinking.

It takes work to ensure that a story reading is successful. As the reception example shows, the teacher has to prepare for the story reading. Even though most teachers are likely to know *The Very Hungry Caterpillar* it is nevertheless worth spending time considering the story reading. We look at this in the next chapter.

3

Reading stories in the classroom: getting started

Reading stories works. And they work even better if the teacher has given some thought to the selection of the book to be read and has prepared for the reading. How will the book be read? Reading the book is a performance and the teacher needs to consider and possibly practice the performance before reading to the children. With the youngest primary school children and pre-schoolers, it is important that the children take part.

Selecting a book to read

This text mentions a small number of children's books. But this barely scratches the surface; there are so many attractive and worthwhile books for reading to children. We can never know for sure which books will especially appeal to any one child. For instance, between the age of 1 and 3, Louie constantly returned to a favourite text *Fix-It Duck* (Alborough, 2001). The readings of this picture book changed over the years. Louie listened to the book being read when he was 1 year old and inserted the rhyming words during his second year. By 3 he knew and had memorised large chunks of the book. He was attracted to the characters of Duck, Sheep, Goat and Frog and was familiar with every minute detail of the illustrations. At times other books became more important to him, such as *The Gruffalo* (Donaldson, 1999), '*Emergency!*' (Mayo, 2002) and many others. But, for whatever reason, *Fix-It Duck* and other Duck books were requested by him at intervals throughout his development in using literacy.

As we see in the next chapter, repetition, rhyme and rhythm are among the key elements that help us to select a particularly suitable book for young children. These attributes are evident in *Fix-It Duck* and may have contributed to Louie's enjoyment. At other times it might be particular happenings in the home, classroom or wider community, or previous experience, that suggest a book to be read. Whatever is the case, the books that are selected have to be good.

Other reasons may prevail when we read a story or chapter book to older primary school children. Again there are many great books waiting to be read. For instance, I have read *Kensuke's Kingdom* (Morpurgo, 1999) to a class of Year 5 children over a two week period. The children were captivated by the story, composed notes that might have been written by Michael and Kensouke, developed a conversation between the two characters – and, incidentally, rapidly conquered speech marks – and found out about geographical and historical aspects of the story. And beyond the picture books, there are many chapter books, waiting to be read.

Preparing for a story reading

Because so many books are available, busy teachers may be tempted to pick one up at the last minute to read aloud to the class. However, experience of reading aloud quickly demonstrates that adequate preparation is needed. Wade (1990) advocates that 'stories need to be introduced, presented, recommended, talked over and savoured together' (p31). This suggests that teachers need to prepare for a story reading just like other aspects of the curriculum.

Graham and Kelly (1997) provide a story reading checklist under four main headings: select, plan, practice, and deliver. For their plan section, Graham and Kelly identify six areas to consider:

- resources that might be needed

- how much is to be read

- how the book will be introduced

- points the teacher might raise for discussion

- how to conclude the session, and

- what might be used if time is available at the end of the read-aloud. (p63)

These issues need not take up much of the teacher's time. But the list does indicate that teachers will need to be well prepared for the story reading.

Trelease (1995) also comments on preparation for story reading, making the point that teachers need to preview the book by reading it to themselves beforehand. This ensures that they know the book and that it is appropriate for the children. Trelease suggests choosing a book that matches the intellectual, social and emotional level of the audience. This is not easy, but teachers will be aware of the books the children enjoy and will become increasingly competent at making the link between text and audience. Gervase Phinn (2000) pays attention to choosing books for children that will be read in the classroom. He shows how many worthwhile texts are available, in his wide selection of stories, poetry and non-fiction. Such lists are helpful, although teachers still need to preview the book for themselves.

The preview ensures that the adult can read the book with an awareness of the flow of the text. Even experienced teachers find that for a story reading to be successful, a practice read is helpful – even when the teacher has already read the book to another class. The practice serves as a reminder of the precise words, the page turning, particular key phrases and the phrases to emphasise. A story reading that is rehearsed is likely to be a worthwhile performance that captures the children's interest. Authors of picture books (such as Julia Donaldson of *The Gruffalo*) report that they read aloud their completed book to make sure that the flow feels right (Lane, 2008). If the author feels the need to do this, so should the story reader.

Reading as a performance

In the real classroom, it may be difficult to get the children settled for a story. Mood is important, and the teacher should try to settle the children without making authoritarian requests for attention. Equally, avoid any threat that there will be no story if the children make too much noise. The story reading is too important to be lost. Neuman (1998) suggests starting with a song, a finger play or a brief chant to signal the time for a story reading. Some teachers use music to set the mood and tone. Once story readings are established as an enjoyable and exciting event in the day, the children are likely to settle down quickly. Their enjoyment is even more assured when children can sense the teacher's enthusiasm for books. Many teachers get the children's attention simply by saying they have another exciting book to read. Then, as Mem Fox (2001) puts it, the voicing of the first line 'should be sensational. The aim is to grab our audience immediately and never let them go' (p48).

Trelease (1995) has further useful suggestions for guaranteeing the quality of the activity: teachers should ensure that all the children can see the pictures easily, sitting with their head just above the children's so their voice will carry to all the children, using plenty of expression and adjusting their pace of reading to fit the story.

Trelease particularly urges teachers to avoid reading too quickly, which he considers to be the commonest mistake. Reading at the right pace, pausing for effect, and appropriate emphasis are all likely to captivate the audience and extend their interest in story and literacy. Mem Fox (2001) lists seven things to do with the voice. Six are contrasts 'loud and soft, fast and slow and high and low' (p42) and the seventh is pausing. So both Trelease and Fox regard pausing as important – and it is important for the children who listen. Mem Fox provides examples from her own books, where the contrasts of voice are made obvious and link directly to the words being read – and she has a web page where those contrasts are demonstrated: www.memfox.net. Reading aloud to children requires a performance that can enhance the words and content of the story.

Ensuring that the children are involved

The interactive aspect of the story reading has many benefits, especially for younger children. We saw how the reading in the reception classroom of *The Very Hungry Caterpillar* elicited comments from the children about the story and illustrations:

John: He nibbles holes.

Amy: I can see the moon.

They also related the text to their own experiences:

Matthew: I like strawberries.

And they demonstrated their knowledge:

Sophie: Real caterpillars eat leaves.

Engaging in talk of this kind enables children to understand the story, extract meanings and clarify their own thinking. The children become 'partners in the telling' (Dombey, 1988, p75) even when they cannot yet read the print and have not seen the book before.

Teachers should not be unnerved by the children's comments and questions during the reading. The pupils' curiosity and interest is fostered when the teacher answers their questions and responds to their comments. Dombey (1988) suggests that the teacher even invite the children to join in the reading as active participants. The reception teacher did this very effectively:

Teacher: I wonder why there are holes in the fruit?

Then later:

Teacher: What else gave it [the caterpillar] a stomach-ache?

Her questions encouraged the children to participate, and their comments demonstrated that they had become used to contributing.

Additionally, the teacher can encourage children to participate in the actual reading of the text, especially the parts where phrases are repeated:

Teacher: *On Monday*
                he ate through
                one apple.
                But [with emphasis and pausing for the children]

Children: *he was still*
                hungry.

Inviting the children into the story reading to speak some of the text encourages them to behave like readers and provides a foundation for their involvement with the book.

After the children have commented and asked questions, the teacher returns to focus on the book and resumes reading. This is not easy. It is done by changing the emphasis in the voice, pausing and using signals for the children, such as 'On the next page' or 'Now'. Most teachers of young children can perfect this skill so that the story reading flows from reading to active participation and back to reading.

The contribution of the teacher is not only verbal. Facial expressions can encourage children to engage or they can suggest a continuation of the story. A finger placed on the lips may indicate a return to the story. These non-verbal behaviours are designed to encourage the children's participation in the story reading, to signal a reading from the book and, in some circumstances, to remind one or more children of the behaviour which is appropriate.

After the reading, the children can be involved by taking part in a class discussion. As Trelease (1995) notes, this gives the children time for their thoughts, hopes, fears and discoveries to surface. He reminds us that such discussions should not be turned into a quiz or an attempt to pry story interpretations from the children. Rather, talking about the book helps them to create meanings (McGee, 1995). The discussion can also be the springboard that takes the children from the story into other activities.

This glimpse inside a reception classroom offers an indication of how teachers might work with young children during a story reading, although story reading will vary according to the age of children. In pre-school, the dialogue between the teacher and children is often longer and less focused than with older children, and the teacher may need to work harder to respond to their comments and use them to return to the reading. Older children may be more willing to listen to the entire story, saving their comments until the end. And their interest in following up aspects of the story in pictures and writing will be more extensive.

Routman (1991) identifies reading stories in the classroom as 'the single most influential factor in young children's success in learning to read' (p32). The interactive nature of story readings provides major support for the children's literacy learning. Through the use of questions and statements from both adult and child, each passage is clarified and integrated with other parts of the story. Young children can anticipate, or predict, upcoming story events through the knowledge they acquire. This experience helps them develop strategies for making inferences and hypotheses both for the book being read and for other written language. The reception children enjoyed the reading of *The Very Hungry Caterpillar*, became involved in the story, participated in a related discussion and used the meanings and the words to extend their excitement into other aspects of learning.

Some teachers may feel uncomfortable about devoting a great deal of time to story reading (Routman, 1991). The children and teacher so enjoy the activity that it may not seem like hard enough work. But the children's enjoyment becomes the basis for learning about stories and reading, learning to read, learning through literacy, and wanting to read (Short, 1999). Because of these numerous benefits, story readings should take place every day – and even more frequently for the youngest children in schools.

4

The importance of narrative
and quality books

Narrative and story are central features in the early years of education (Whitehead, 1987). A particular benefit of story is that it provides a way of organising thinking about experiences and making them meaningful. Bruner (1968) argues that there are two modes of thought, 'a good story and a well-formed argument' (p99). These provide different ways of viewing reality. Although both are important, this book focuses on narrative.

As children 'transact' or interact with stories (Rosenblatt, 1978), they consider the development of the action and begin to become aware of what the protagonists and antagonists involved in the action know, think or feel. These transactions enable children to build what Langer (1995) refers to as an envisionment; that is, the understanding they have about the text. As ideas unfold and new ideas come to mind, this envisionment, or understanding, is subject to change. During a reading the story is a basis for encouraging thinking as the children interact with the adult. For example, we saw in Chapter 2 how, as the children heard multiple readings of *The Very Hungry Caterpillar* and engaged in activities related to the story, they extended their thinking and developed their ideas.

Whitehead (1997) reminds us that pleasure is 'the first and all-pervasive theme in the world of literature' (p119). This pleasure is evident in classrooms where teachers and children share stories, particularly in classrooms where an initial emphasis on the story is key. Following the story with related activities, as shown in Chapter 2, can add to the children's enjoyment. However, we must remember that such activities must 'not detract from children's enjoyment of good books' (Lane and Wright, 2007, p674).

When the story gives pleasure, play and learning come naturally and inevitably, as the children construct meaning about what they have heard and considered. Dorothy White (1954/1984) offers numerous examples of how her pre-school daughter Carol used a story line as the basis for her play at home. For instance, when Carol was almost 4 years old, Dorothy read her a book titled *The Little Train* (Lenski, 1946), in which the key character is Engineer Small, whose job is to ensure that the train is ready for its journey. Carol regularly 'played trains' after hearing this story: 'Carol oils wheels, shovels coal, reads her orders, pulls a whistle-cord and makes off from the sofa station for the tunnel under the table' (White, p83). From this play, Carol was able to extend her understanding of railways and construct her own meanings onto the story. Phillips and McNaughton (1990) suggest that children who have had frequent storybook readings at home learn how to construct meaning from unfamiliar texts.

Whitehead (1987) suggests that there are three main strands to support the claims that narrative and story benefit young children – skills, cultural heritage, and personal development. These strands are interrelated and often all three are apparent at once.

Skills

Children who have a substantial number of encounters with books at home learn in their first few years how to manipulate and use a book. In a longitudinal study of story readings with my granddaughter Alice, I noted that by age 12 months,

Alice could handle a book by:
picking it up or extracting one from a bookshelf,
orienting the book correctly so it was the right way up,
turning a page when she wanted to look at the next picture,
turn the pages from the front towards the back.
(Campbell, 1999, p17)

This competence is typical of many children who have similar opportunities to explore books: they see demonstrations of reading by adults and are supported by adults as they manipulate books. In the classroom, the adult demonstrations that occur naturally as part of reading a story ensure that even children with little experience of books learn these skills.

Children also learn about the language of print from stories, and they acquire understanding of the structure of stories – beginning, middle, and end – as well as understanding about characters, setting and plot. Carol Fox (1993) provides evidence of this learning in her study of the oral storytelling of five pre-school children. Transcripts of these retellings demonstrate the children's learning. For instance, Fox notes that when Justine was 4 years 1 month old, she related the following story:

Once upon a time there were two little dicky birds in a tree
and mammy one said 'Don't go out there'
but the naughtiest was the little baby one
he went out 'cos he didn't listen to his mum
she said 'There's wolves out there and foxes and
ugly lions and other sorts of things that will
eat the birds and crawling insects and
spiders and witches'
and he flyed out of the nest
and one of the tigers opened his mouth and
gobbled him all up
and the second little baby came to eat him up
and that's the end of the story. (p85)

In her detailed analysis of this story, Fox notes that the actions happen in the past tense and the mother bird speaks in the present tense. Although this is a simple story structure, it contains two actions and causal resolutions, and it was not Justine's richest narrative. This example of storytelling and others like it demonstrate a wealth of learning about language.

Children can extend their understanding of language when they have the opportunity to write about aspects of the stories they've heard an adult read aloud or rewrite the stories in their own words. Additionally, children learn about letters and letter-sound relationships from stories (see Chapter 4). However when we look at the story writing of 5-year-old Dylan (Figure 8) we see how

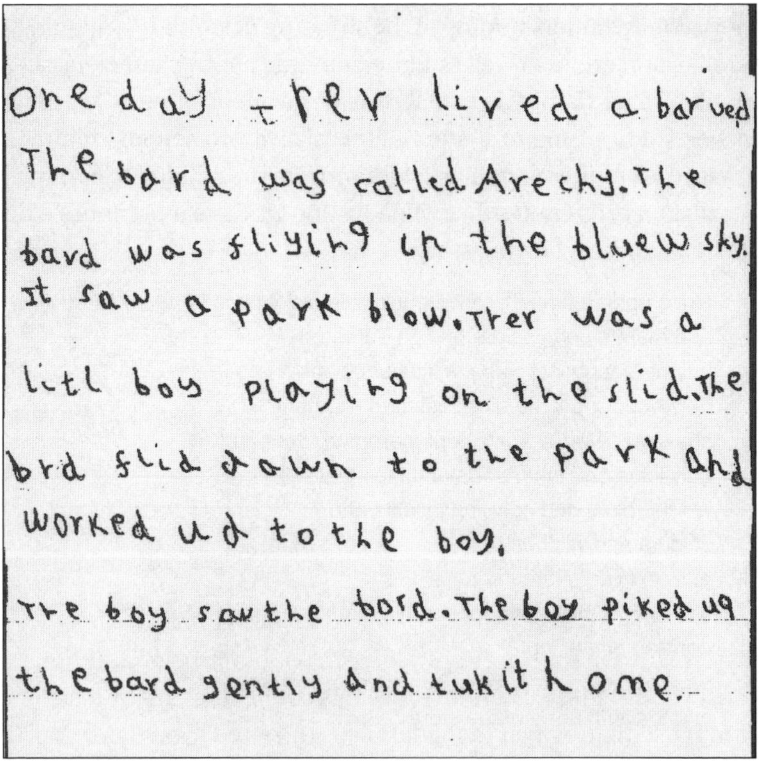

One day tfer lived a barved The bard was called Arechy. The bard was fliying in the bluew sky. It saw a park blow. Trer was a litl boy playirg on the slid. The brd slid down to the park and worked ud to the boy.

Tre boy saw the bord. The boy piked uq the bard gentiy and tuk it home.

Figure 8: Arechy Bird

much he too has learned about story structure, the use of two main characters and the resolution to the story. And we also see the extent to which, given the opportunity to write freely, he tries to use his knowledge of letters and sounds to create the words that he wants to include.

Dylan was able to write numerous words conventionally but others are clearly developmental or invented spellings. He attempted a number of different ways to write 'bird' without quite getting it right by the end of the story, and his attempts at 'up' were illuminating. Each invented spelling enables us to detect the way in which the written word might have been created from his knowledge of letter and sound.

Cultural heritage

Children learn about a wider world from narrative, especially through the oral tradition of nursery rhymes, singing games and chants (Opie and Opie, 1959), as well as the folk tales and fairy tales that are handed from one generation to another. Then there is the 'received' literature (Whitehead, 1987), which includes books that are read in successive generations and serve as a link to our past.

When children engage with the narrative of nursery rhymes, they enjoy the rhythm and rhyme. They learn about story structure and acquire understanding of onset and rime, which teachers can capitalise on later. And nursery rhymes often suggest links with the past:

> Ring-ring o'roses
> A pocket full of posies.
> A-tishoo! A-tishoo!
> We all fall down.

This rhyme is a startling reminder of the bubonic plague. Although most young children cannot make this connection, many teachers find it useful to return to the familiar nursery rhymes later at primary school and explore the origins of the rhyme.

Children are likely to meet some fairy tales in a variety of formats. For instance, Janet and Allan Ahlberg's (1978) *Each Peach Pear Plum*, makes only brief reference to key characters:

> *Cinderella on the stairs*
> *I spy the Three Bears*

Nevertheless, the detailed pictures beside each rhyme encourage young children to think and talk about these characters, and this can lead to extended readings of the fairy tales from other books.

In recent years, certain picture books have become part of a new collection of received literature. Famously, *The Very Hungry Caterpillar* (Carle, 1969) has been read aloud with, and read by, millions of children around the world. It is read to children by parents who enjoyed it in their own childhood and it still appears to captivate children today. Not only is it part of a received literature but it also expands a child's world. The story of the life cycle is learned alongside the tale about the hungry caterpillar.

Tizard and Hughes (1984) examine the responses of 4-year-old Rosy, who was sharing a book with her mother and thus exploring aspects of a wider world. The title of the book is not indicated, but the plot involves a puffin that witnesses a shipwreck. Here is a portion of the transcript:

Child: Do, um boats, when they're on, right on the sea break like that?

Mother: Well, not very often, but sometimes they do. If the weather's very bad, and they get thrown against the rocks, they do break up. (p63)

Because the family was planning a summer holiday from England to France, Rosy found this response unsettling:

Child: I, I, I, don't want to. I'm not going, but we won't go on, if there's too many people on the boat we won't go on it, will we? (p63)

Rosy talked about boats, discussed the possibility of shipwrecks, and made a connection to a possible sea trip. Such explorations clarify children's thinking and help them 'develop a much richer mental model of the world' (Wells, 1986, p152), which further emphasises the importance of story readings at home and in school.

Personal development

A number of educators have written about the power of stories and the importance of narrative for young children. For example, Kirby (1995) writes,

> The power of stories lies in the opportunities they provide for extending
> children's thinking and feeling in numerous ways including:
> their beliefs, assumptions, attitudes, values about life, situations and people;
> their thinking and responses to everyday life and complex issues;
> their concerns, fears, pain, growing up, feelings and compassion for others;
> their relationships with other people;
> their knowledge of and responses to both their own culture and the culture of others;
>
> their imagination, enjoyment and satisfaction;
> their abilities to predict, question, hypothesise about situations and people;
> the power to create and shape through their own stories;
> the opportunity to talk to adults and peers about stories in an atmosphere
> which is collaborative, supportive and 'risk free'. (p7-8)

Such a substantial list suggests a wider area of learning beyond helping children become readers. And it considers the many aspects of thinking and feeling that are supported by narrative.

I noted this intellectual and emotional engagement as my granddaughter Alice gave a memorised reading of *Sniff-Snuff-Snap!* by Dodd (1995) (Campbell, 1999). The plot involves a warthog restricting the use of a waterhole by other animals. After chasing the animals away, the warthog always returns to the waterhole. At the age of 4 years 7 months, Alice relied on her memory of previous story readings and was able to recite the correct words about the warthog's last return as we looked at the final pages of the book:

Alice: *Back came the warthog,*
          tired and hot,
          for a long,
          cool drink
          at his favourite spot.
          Down past rocks
          and thornbush tree,
          he came to the waterhole
          BUT
          what did he see?
          THICK
          BROWN
          MUD.
   (Campbell, 1999, p107)

Alice then illustrated her thinking about the story and her feelings about the warthog by adding a last few lines. In the final picture a drop of rain splashes on to the warthog's back. So Alice added,

          Drip, drop, drip.
          The rain came down
          and filled up the waterhole again. (p108)

In creating that ending, Alice demonstrated empathy for the warthog. She was also thinking through the consequences of the rainfall in that arid environment. Interestingly, her first line re-captures the rhythm of the title of the story by using the *dr* consonant blend. The frequent parent-child and grandparent-child story readings of this book had enabled the young reader to gain ownership of the words. This supported her development toward becoming an independent reader. And the quality of the narrative did far more for Alice: it encouraged her thinking and feelings about the characters and the plot, to which she responded so creatively.

Numerous observations have been made about how narrative supports personal development. Wade (1990) refers to the sustenance of story, noting that quality texts provide 'food for the mind and for the feelings' (p30). Evans (1998) explores children's thoughtful responses to key emotional issues in some stories. In one instance, she studied year 2 children as they wrote about the death of a pet dog in response to a reading of the story *I'll Always Love You* (Wilhelm, 1985). The children discussed the sad parts of the story and related it to their own experiences' concluding that although the death of Elfie, the dog, was sad, the story as a whole was not, because the dog had had a good life.

The intellectual and emotional sustenance children receive from a story makes them want to go on reading (Bettelheim and Zelan, 1981). Ensuring that children want to continue reading, to move to other books and to reflect on what is read is an aim for all teachers.

Books of quality

There are so many good books written for young children that one can only mention a few. Excellent books which are cited frequently in *Reading stories with young children* include those by outstanding authors four different English-speaking countries: Eric Carle from the United States; Lynley Dodd from New Zealand; Mem Fox, whose writing is centred on Australia; and Pat Hutchins from the United Kingdom. This still does no more than touch the surface of the wealth of worthwhile books that can be shared with young children.

A much wider range of books for young children is listed in various sources. In Trelease's (1995) *The Read-Aloud Handbook*, over 100 pages are devoted to an annotated list of books that can be read aloud and Cullinan's (1989) annotated list appears in a chapter on literature for young children. Routman's *Invitations* (1991) lists books that invite readers into print and identifies predictable books that help children develop early reading strategies as discussed below. Professional journals such as *The Reading Teacher* often feature lists of appropriate recent books to share with young children; a regular column on children's books started in September 1999 (Giorgis and Johnson, 1999), and includes lists of books for reading aloud. The columnists also group books for particular purposes, such as 'for inviting interaction' (p80). *English four to eleven* too has regular reviews of books for children. On the internet booktrustchilrensbooks.org.uk and several other sites provide information on children's literature (Karchmer, 2000). Teachers can stay up to date by checking the annual awards given to outstanding books for young children.

Predictable books

Rhodes (1981) argues for the value of predictability in books for young children. Certain books enable young children at school to read right away, because they draw on the children's knowledge of language and of the world. She maintains that when the 'language flows naturally, and the vocabulary and content reflect what children know' (p513), children can predict what the author is going to say and how it will be said.

According to Rhodes, the key characteristic of predictability is the use of repetitive patterns. For example, *Slinki Malinki, Open the Door* (Dodd, 1993) relates the mischievous adventures of the cat, Slinki Malinki and a parrot. After each room they visit the text repeats the rhyme:

> *Slinki Malinki*
> *jumped high off the floor,*
> *he swung on a handle*
> *and opened*
> *a door.*

Children hearing this book in a read-aloud can soon predict the next page and prepare for the havoc the cat and the parrot will wreak in the next room.

Predictable books are characterised by familiar concepts, a symbiotic match of text to illustrations, rhyme, rhythm of language, the familiarity of the story or story line to the child, and the use of familiar sequences (Rhodes, 1981). What does this mean when books such as Slinki Malinki are read in a classroom? Children already know that cats may make a mess at home, so this story involves familiar concepts and thus assists their understanding. The close match between the text and illustrations also supports the predictability.

Children bring their knowledge to school. Many arrive with some knowledge of folk tales, fairy tales and songs. When they meet Cinderella again, the familiarity of the characters aids the predictability. Some multilayered texts (Watson, 1993) make use of that familiarity. As noted earlier, in *Each Peach Pear Plum* (Ahlberg and Ahlberg, 1978) the characters from one familiar text meet characters *from* other texts:

> *Cinderella on the stairs*
> *I spy the Three Bears*

This theme runs throughout the story.

We saw how Eric Carle used the familiar sequence of numbers from 1 to 5 and the days of the week in *The Very Hungry Caterpillar*. The two sequences are linked as the caterpillar eats his way through the fruit on each day of the week. The children bring some understanding of these familiar sequences to the story reading, and the story further develops their understanding and aids their prediction of what is to come. The children's knowledge of language and the world helps them create meanings from books, and the repetition, rhyme, and rhythm of the text – what Wade (1990) calls 'the three R's' of language and story (p7) – support the young children's learning.

Repetition

Repetition that contributes to the story line helps children become good readers. Typically, the repetition is of a phrase or sentence rather than a single word, as in some reading schemes used in the past. In *Slinki Malinki, Open the Door,* the repeated sentence contributes greatly to the excitement of the story and the build-up to its conclusion. The phrase appears six times on six of the 15 pages of print. The repetition also aids children when they begin to read such texts for themselves.

Because the repeated phrase or sentence is an integral part of the story, children pick up the phrase very quickly. For instance, when Alice was 2 years 9 months old, it took just one reading at home of *Good-Night Owl* (Hutchins, 1972) before she contributed a key repetition:

Grandfather:	*Owl*
Alice:	*tried to sleep.*
Grandfather:	*The bees buzzed,*
	buzz buzz,
	and
Alice:	*owl tried to sleep.*

(Campbell, 1999, p59)

Although Alice had not yet begun to give much attention to the print in books, she did use that key phrase when she tried to construct the story by herself immediately after hearing the story for a second time:

Alice:	*Owl tried to sleep*
	There's the bees,
	Owl tried to sleep
	and
	the bees buzzed
	buzz buzz.
	Owl tried to sleep
	and the squirrel was sitting in the tree.

It is not only girls who listen attentively to story at that age and learn by heart much of the content. Louie at 2 years 8 months had absorbed much of the book '*Emergency!*' (Mayo, 2002) during the frequent repeat readings he requested. So that as his grandfather read to, and with, him Louie made a major contribution to the story reading, using his knowledge of the repeated words and story rhythm.

Grandfather *Ambulance speeding*

Louie   *emergency!*

    Whee-oww! Whee-oww! Pull over, make way!

    Siren screaming, light beam-beaming.

Grandfather *Help is coming –*

Louie *it's on the way!*

While repetition contributes to this story line, it also builds up the predictability and helps children toward ownership of the text. In addition, it supports young readers when they attempt to construct the story for themselves or move toward reading a well-known book on their own.

Rhyme

A number of picture books include a rhyme element, which children generally love. For instance, in Hairy Maclary from Donaldson's Dairy (Dodd, 1983), the main characters are introduced one by one in an extending rhyme:

> *Schnitzel von Krumm*
> *with a very low tum,*
> *Bitzer Maloney*
> *all skinny and bony,*
> *Muffin McLay*
> *like a bundle of hay,*
> *Bottomley Potts*

> *covered in spots,*
> *Hercules Morse*
> *as big as a horse*
> *and Hairy Maclary*
> *from Donaldson's dairy.*

Young children greatly enjoy this story, and they are usually keen to join in with the rhyme within minutes. It is not surprising that after a reading they can be heard using the rhymes as they engage with other activities in the classroom. And any sighting of a Dalmatian dog is almost certain to evoke the words 'Bottomley Potts covered in spots.'

Not only do children like to hear rhymes, they also enjoy playing with words and using them to create their own rhymes or jingles (Chukovsky, 1963). Teachers can capitalise on this interest in the classroom, first by providing worthwhile books for story readings and then by using their learning as a basis for phonological development. As Meek (1990) indicates, when children have fun with rhymes, phonology is developed. For example, with *Hairy Maclary from Donaldson's Dairy*, the play with rhyme leads to an awareness of onset such as (*m* and *h*) and rime (*-orse*), as in *Morse* and *horse*. This awareness, Goswami and Bryant (1990) suggest, is significant feature of children's development as readers.

A brief look at a few lines from one of Dr. Seuss's books, such as *Green Eggs and Ham* (1960), illustrates how children will be made aware of onset and rime:

> *That Sam-I-am!*
> *That Sam-I-am!*
> *I do not like*
> *that Sam-I-am!*
> *Do you like*
> *green eggs and ham?*

And later in the rhyme:

Would you eat them
in a box?
Would you eat them
with a fox?

In the first instance, the rime element -*am* together with the onset letters *S* and *h* become part of the children's language and awareness. The rime -*ox* together with the onset *b* and *f* are among the many others that follow. But mainly the children enjoy the nonsense of the repeating rhyme throughout the book.

Rhythm

Rhythm is an important feature of books for young children. The use of rhyme and repetition in *Green Eggs and Ham* creates a rhythm that children listen to and like to use for themselves. It is doubtful whether this book is ever read aloud without the words being delivered in an almost song-like rhythm with the words. Children enjoy the rhythms that are created by the repetition and rhyme.

Rhythm in stories also appeals to children, and is produced in a various ways in the books that are read aloud. In *The Very Hungry Caterpillar*, a two-page spread highlights the foods the caterpillar ate on Saturday:

On Saturday
he ate through
one piece of
chocolate cake,
one ice-cream cone,
one pickle,
one slice of Swiss cheese,
one slice of salami...

The repetition of *one* on this first page of text is repeated another five times on the opposite page as other foods are introduced. However, it is the listing of the foods that appears to give the rhythm to the text. The alliteration, such as *slice of salami*, adds a rhythmic feel to the text and attracts the children to the words.

The image created by the sounds in *slice of salami* can remain prominent in children's minds. In a classroom, of 5 year-old children (Campbell, 1992), I observed Richard read Carle's book to his teacher in an individual reading conference. The correct reading of each miscue follows in parentheses:

Richard: *one slice of salami (Swiss) cheese*
             one slice of salami
             one lollipop

and then at the end of that double page

             one slice of salami (watermelon). (p24)

Richard miscued Swiss and watermelon as the memory and rhythm of *slice of salami* dominated part of his reading.

Fox (1993) notes the importance of rhythm in some of the storytelling of pre-schoolers. One of the children in her study, Josh, regularly heard weather reports on the radio which described conditions at sea at Fair Isle, Dogger Bank, and Rockall and elsewhere. Josh caught the rhythm of those broadcasts and enjoyed producing his own weather reports.

Many teachers of young children seek predictability, repetition, rhyme, and rhythm in the books they read to the children. Others suggest different criteria for quality books. Nutbrown (1994) maintains that children's books should be evaluated according to their appeal, readability, content, development and inclusivity. Hart-Hewins and Wells (1990) suggest a somewhat similar list, namely: content, language, attractiveness, and ease of reading. Teachers can add their own criteria to such lists based on their experience of reading to children and their discussion with colleagues about books. Many factors need to be taken into account when selecting books for reading to and with young children.

Poetry and non-fiction

The emphasis in this chapter has been on the importance of narrative and children's engagement with stories through the use of high-quality storybooks for story readings at home and school. However, teachers of young children know poetry and non-fiction also have an important place in readings aloud.

Some of the stories that are read to children might be regarded as extended poems. The rhyme and rhythm of many nursery rhymes, songs, and stories that are read aloud to children ensure that they will also enjoy hearing poetry read aloud. From readings, children often like to move on to reading other poetry and writing their own simple rhymes and poems.

Many stories communicate facts. For instance, *Cimru the Seal* (Radcliffe, 1997) provides information beyond the story about the life of a seal, its diet and predators. The children learn much of that information incidentally, as the story is read aloud. However, in a Year 2 classroom I observed, a discussion after the story was read demonstrated that the children were interested in exploring the factual aspects of the text. So it important that from time to time teachers choose non-fiction books, or sections from them, as read-alouds. The children then have a model of scientific writing, and they can consider the 'well-formed argument' (Bruner, 1968, p99).

The many different books that are read to and with children will interest and excite them. The story readings, and the activities that are linked to them, also facilitate the children's reading and writing. At the same time, the children also learn about print features (Wolf, 2008). This is the subject of Chapter 5.

5

Reading stories and
print features

The range of excellent storybooks available for reading aloud enables young children to experience the widest possible contact with letters, sounds and spellings. Studies of young children who regularly have stories read to them at home indicate that they move on to school with a strong foundation of graphophonic knowledge (Campbell, 2004). The miscues these children produce as they read and the invented spellings they create as they write are indicators of this knowledge. For children in the early years of primary school, reading stories in the classroom provide a similar opportunity to learn about the alphabet, phonics and spelling. As Kane (1999) argues, phonics can and should be taught from meaningful contexts: 'The quality children's literature we want our children immersed in provides all the examples of phonics enthusiasts could ever want' (p771).

Just the titles of books such as *Hop on Pop* (Seuss, 1963) hint at the learning that is likely to take place as such books are shared with children. Part of this story rhyme reads,

> *We like to hop.*
> *We like to hop*
> *on top of Pop.*

STOP

> *You must not*
> *hop on Pop.*

As children explore and think about writing, their awareness of sounds is enhanced. Singing, reciting, writing and playing with words such as *hop, Pop, top* and *stop* makes that so. As Strickland (1998) suggests, the children's involvement in rhymes, songs, and alliteration in various links to story readings promotes phonemic awareness. It also provides the basis for learning the letters of the alphabet, phonics and spelling.

Alphabet

Powell and Hornsby (1998) demonstrate that children using literature in a reception class can consider graphophonic connections in a meaningful way. They show how one teacher used text from the storybook *Possum Magic* (Fox, 1983) to help the children think about a letter and then create an alliteration. The book reads:

> *Later, on a beach in Perth, they ate a piece of pavlova.*
> *Hush's legs appeared. So did her body.*
> *'You look wonderful, you precious possum!' said Grandma Poss.*

The teacher and the children used the alliteration to create a tongue twister: *The precious possum had a piece of pavlova in Perth.*

Over a few days the teacher developed a chart of *p* words, starting with words from the story, and the children suggested other words to add to the list. Together they created a word wall that used words from the story reading, children's forenames and other words they found important: *Perth, pavlova, precious, possum, Patrick, party, puppy, Paul* and *pink* (p86).

Staying with the theme, the teacher selected poems such as 'Peter, Peter, Pumpkin Eater' to extend the children's attention to the letter. The <Pp> letter chart (showing both uppercase and lower-case letters) was hung on the wall for the children to add other words beginning with *p*.

The class went on to develop the link with the story. As the pos-sums continue their journey around Australia eating 'people food,' the story reveals that:

> *They ate Anzac biscuits in Adelaide,*
> *mornay and Minties in Melbourne,*
> *steak and salad in Sydney,*
> *and pumpkin scones in Brisbane.*

Powell and Hornsby show how the first two lines formed the basis for two other letter charts. Again, the teacher began with words from the story and then added words from the children. Such activities helped them learn the letters of the alphabet and move beyond it to detailed consideration of the letters.

Non-fiction alphabet books, such as *Animalia* (Base, 1986), can add to the children's learning when they are used as the basis for a story reading. As Strickland (1998) notes, making alphabet books readily available in the classroom for the children to browse through after reading it aloud furthers their interest and supports their learning.

Phonics

The fact that the children are learning phonics from story readings and follow-up activities is evident in numerous ways. For instance, during one reception story reading of *When I Was Little Like You* (Walsh, 1997), one of the 5-year-olds in the class made an un-expected comment:

Teacher: *'When I was little like you,' said Gran,*
            'we bought fish from the boatman on the

> *quay. A brace of bright mackerel for*
> *supper, still fresh and shining.'*

Francis: You get a /k/ with three letters. Like in *quay*. You can have a *k*, *c*, or *q*.

The teacher had not taught these letters and letter sounds directly, but the constant play with language, words and letters ensured that they were learned. The story reading led to a consideration of initial letter-sound correspondences and thinking about some words. It also gave the children a chance to initiate discussions about letter sounds.

In one first year classroom, the teacher read aloud the Big Book version of *Walking Through the Jungle* (Lacome, 1993), and encouraged the children to write a sentence using alliteration. Some of the children chose an animal from the story, such as the crocodile (see Figure 9).

In this writing, the child was able to produce alliteration by spelling each word conventionally, although substituting *an* for *a*. Other children wrote about animals that were not part of the story, such as a flamingo (see Figure 10).

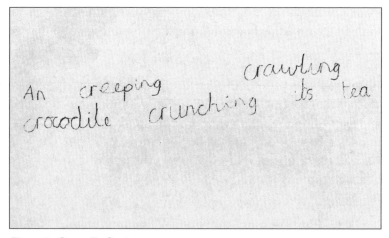

Figure 9 : Crocodile Sentence

A. fluffy flmego fluffying it's feathers.

Figure 10: Flamingo Sentence

Although *fluffying* may not be a recognised word, here it appears to fit well with the child's description of it. As the word *flamingo* was not part of the story, it had to be written unseen and the child demonstrated knowledge of letters and sounds and a willingness to construct words using this knowledge. When children are encouraged to write following story readings – and when their spellings are acknowledged for the learning that is demonstrated – the foundations are in place for conventional spelling to develop, especially when the teacher and the children talk freely about letters, sounds and words in context. As Geekie, Cambourne and Fitzsimmons (1999) note, when children are encouraged to write from the very beginning of schooling, the need for the explicit teaching of phonics is reduced.

The alliterative writing activity, like many other literacy activities, encouraged the children to think about letters and sounds in the context of a story they enjoyed. The extended alliteration that is contained in Margaret Attwood's *Princess Prunella and the Purple Peanut* (1995) is typically enjoyed by older primary children. In one year five classroom the children discussed the writing and then proceeded to write their own alliterative stories. The extent of the children's enjoyment and understanding is illustrated in these few sentences from one of their stories:

> *Pretty puppy eats lots of portions of pies and for pudding a plum.*
> *She is now getting very plump. Pretty puppy likes to pounce*
> *on people, she pulls and pushes a lot.*

Such writing is creative. Stimulated by the story reading, it fosters a clear understanding of alliteration and encourages the children to play with words, letters and sounds, and language.

There are numerous ways in which children can explore letters and sounds creatively. Opitz (2000) provides guidance about the possibilities suggesting various books that can serve as the basis for exploring alliteration and other aspects of letter-sound correspondences naturally, as the stories are read aloud.

When children are encouraged to write in a variety of formats, they develop an understanding of phonics and a love of writing. Phinn (2000) suggests that young children should both listen to and write poems. Miniature poems, such as the Japanese haiku, are manageable for children because they are short. Children in years two and three respond well to the discipline of the haiku's short lines of five, seven, and five syllables. It requires them to think carefully about letters and sounds as they consider the syllables in each word. This builds on earlier work they may have done in pre-school and reception classrooms to clap out the syllables in their names and in nursery rhymes (Ericson and Juliebö, 1998).

Word wall

The walls of the classrooms for young children traditionally carry a great deal of print. As long ago as 1958 the many pictures in Goddard's book on infant school reading show simple print being used to support children's reading and writing. Goddard argued that just having the print on the wall is not enough; the teacher has to talk about it with the children.

Goddard's children also had their own 'wordbooks' or individual dictionaries. Throughout the year, the children expanded them, adding words from the classroom print and reading books, and words they asked the teacher to help them spell correctly. The strategy supported children with a personal resource for words they might otherwise have difficulty with. But the teacher could not always prevent the dictionaries from becoming overloaded with words that were seldom used. Neither could she support every child as needed and some important words were probably missed. Providing a classroom dictionary or word wall tries to overcome such difficulties.

Cunningham and Allington (1999) argue for word walls in reception and primary classrooms but they too point out that it is not enough for the teacher to hang a word wall in the classroom and suggest that the children use it as necessary. Instead, these authors argue, it is important for the teachers to 'DO' word walls. In particular, they suggest that the teacher should:

- be selective and 'stingy' about what words go up there, limiting the words to those really common words that children need a lot in writing

- add words gradually – five a week

- make them accessible by putting them where everyone can see them, writing them in big black letters, and using a variety of colours so that words which are constantly confused (*for, from, that, them, they, this*, etc.) are in different colours.

■ practice the words by chanting and writing them because struggling readers are seldom good at visual learning and can't just look at words and remember them

■ do a variety of review activities to provide enough practice so the children can read and spell the words instantly and automatically

■ make sure that word-wall words are spelled correctly in all their writing. (adapted from Cunningham and Allington, 1999, p136)

The first and last points stress the need for the teacher to be very selective in the words they choose. Their expectations can support the children in learning key high-frequency words and so facilitate their reading and writing.

Many reception teachers start by placing each child's forename in the word wall in alphabetic order, which has a section for each letter of the alphabet. Studies of individual children before they start school emphasise the importance of their ability to write their own name (Baghban, 1984; Campbell, 1999; Schickedanz, 1990) and the children are interested in seeing their name on the wall. The class can also make comparisons from the listings. For example, it would be remarkable if there were not at least two children with forenames starting with the same letter. Then the teacher can expand the list by adding some of the key characters from storybooks or some high-frequency words, as suggested by Cunningham and Allington (1999). The word wall supports the children's learning of the alphabet, recognition of each letter and phonic knowledge of initial letter sounds.

Moustafa (1997) also advocates the use of word walls, suggesting that they be created specifically from the predictable stories that are read aloud in class. In this case, the teacher asks the children to choose their favourite words from the story after reading a story several times. The children will be supported further if the teacher places a picture from the story, perhaps of the key character, next to each word.

Additionally, the teacher can highlight certain letters of each word to emphasise the onset or rime – which is an important part of children's learning (Goswami, 1999). For a Humpty-Dumpty story with the words *wall* and *fall*, the teacher might highlight the onset /w/ or /f/, or the rime element /all/. The words can be regrouped frequently as the teacher talks with the children about words starting with /w/, or when the class is considering other /all/ rimes. As Moustafa (1997) indicates, such strategies make the phonics instruction 'explicit, systematic and extensive' (p93).

For Moustafa, working in this way creates a whole-to-parts phonic instruction. However, it differs from traditional phonics instruction, or the return of synthetic phonics into the classroom (Rose, 2006), in that it follows, rather than precedes, the story. It is only after a story has been read to, with, and by children that parts of the words are taught. And it concentrates on units of the syllable – namely, letter-onset and letter-rime correspondences – rather than letter-phoneme correspondences.

Whichever approach is used, the word walls provide support in a number of ways:

■ the children will learn about the letters of the alphabet as each section has a space available for words to be added

■ the sequence of the alphabet is shown by the word wall and the teacher can bring the children's attention to that feature (as well as singing some of the well-known alphabet songs)

■ the high-frequency key words can become part of child's visual memory of words

■ words of interest from the story come from the children and mean something to them so can be learned more readily (Ashton-Warner, 1963)

■ the children learn about word families, first at the level of initial letter similarity and then when the word wall is developed with onset and rime highlighted.

Spelling

Teachers of young children may be concerned lest the use of the word wall might reduce the children's use of invented spellings. If numerous words are displayed, the children have less need to go through the process of sounding out the word to work out how to represent it in print. So teachers need to use word walls with thoughtfully. The children's engagement with invented spellings is too precious to lose.

Interestingly, invented spelling is one of the key links between whole language and phonic-based views of early reading development. Goodman (1990) explores how children are active constructors of knowledge. Invented spelling not only tells us about what they know but also shows how they are constructing literacy from their increasingly sophisticated understanding of print conventions. Adams (1990), although from a different perspective, also values invented spellings:

> In overview, classroom encouragement of invented spellings and independent writing from the start seems a promising approach towards the development of literacy skills. Beyond all that was mentioned above and whether the children are directing their efforts towards good descriptions or imaginative stories, this approach appears incomparable for purposes of developing their abilities to reflect on their own thoughts, to elaborate and organise their ideas, and to express themselves in print. (p386-387)

The teacher will want to support young children in their understanding of print and the production of words in their writing. The word wall can support the children in these endeavours as it helps to create for each child a visual memory of some key and frequently used words that they can then write automatically and conventionally. But teachers will want to ensure that for much of the time, and with many words, the children are actively engaged in constructing the word themselves, using their knowledge of letters and sounds. Initially, this produces invented rather than conventional spellings. It also lays the foundations of literacy knowledge that will serve the children well in the future.

Knowledge of letters, phonics and spelling are all developed from story readings and associated literacy activities such as writing, which arise naturally from those readings. Young children learn about print features because they are immersed in language and literacy. Teachers can support and guide this learning as they talk about print before and after they enjoy hearing stories read to them.

6

Activities based on reading stories

Some teachers read a story with their class early in the day; Hart-Hewins and Wells (1990) for instance often schedule the story reading time just before the children's work period. This allows the teachers to suggest activities that link the story with the children's play, writing and art. Drawing and writing about books helps children understand and think through the stories. When teachers choose books of quality most children are inclined to follow the reading by responding in some way, be it through role-play, drawing, writing, making a book, constructing a model, creating and using a puppet, or learning a song. The forms of response will vary, but some response is likely.

It is clear that a wide range of activities, or 'enterprises' as Routman (1991) calls them, can be developed from stories that are read to and with children. However, it is essential that the stories remain paramount and the other activities and learning are derived naturally from them. Not every book should be linked into the work of the class. Nevertheless, the teacher should be aware of the activities that can be generated by each story, and use the children's enthusiasm and enjoyment of the story as a guide to the activities that are provided or suggested.

For instance, before she read *The Snail and the Whale* (Donaldson, 2003) to the class, a Year 1 teacher considered possible avenues for development. She mapped these possibilities into a subject web (see Figure 11).

The teacher did not use all these activities but took account of used the interests of the children to determine which of them to follow up. But as the children explored the story, the web reminded the teacher of other possibilities. Often the story leads to other stories or one like *The Snail and the Cherry Tree* (Dalgleish, 1990) might introduce a scientific consideration of snails. Whatever avenue is chosen, many teachers follow a story reading by supporting the children's explorations of the story in various ways. The examples that follow come from different classrooms and age groups and feature a range of stories.

Role play

Young children use the stories they have heard in their play activities in the classroom quite naturally (Carter, 1999). Teachers can support children's learning by linking a role play area to a recent story, by for instance arranging a corner to resemble a cave after the class reads *Can't You Sleep, Little Bear?* (Waddell, 1988). The story begins:

> *'Can't you sleep, Little Bear?'*
> *asked Big Bear, putting down his Bear Book*
> *(which was just getting to the interesting part) and*
> *padding over to the bed.*
> *'I'm scared,' said Little Bear.*
> *'Why are you scared, Little Bear?' asked Big Bear.*
> *'I don't like the dark,' said Little Bear.*

During the role play, the children can act out aspects of the story, and in this instance revisit their own concerns, such as fear of the dark. And because this book contains positive literacy images as Big Bear reads a book, the teacher can place a small collection of books in the cave to support the play. And there are other Big Bear

English
Story reading
Discuss pictures
Discuss story
Oral retelling
Writing own version
Alphabet book (word wall)
Sounds for letters
Non-fiction snail/whale books
Writing rhyming silvery trails
Other sea/snail stories

Art/Craft
Frieze of harbour scene
Fish shapes
3 dimensional models
Volcano paintings
Collages

Music
Loud and soft sounds
Moving to different sounds
Rescue vehicle sounds

The Snail and the Whale

Science
Rescue vehicles - helicopters
Float - sink properties
Exploring cranes – lifting heavy objects
Lighthouses

Geography
Map of whale journey – world maps
Go on own mini journey - map
Harbours
Sea routes
Hot lands –cold lands

P.E. / Dance
Move as sea creatures
Move as snail
Fast - slow

History
Development of rescue services
Ships of different times
Lighthouses – past and present

Donaldson, J. (2003) *The Snail and the Whale* London: Macmillan

Subject web for The Snail and the Whale

Figure 11: Subject web for The Snail and the Whale

books to be read with the class eg *Let's go home little bear* (Waddell, 1991).

Hall and Robinson (1985) suggest that the use of storybooks with literacy-based images may contribute to children's understanding of reading and writing. However, it is the characters and events of the stories that provide such a strong basis for the children's play. As White (1954) indicates in relation to her daughter Carol's play at home, 'How these children's books take hold and inhabit her mind!' (p164). Stories do indeed capture the children's minds, extend their imagination, and support role-play.

Adult involvement in the role-play can vary from just reading the story to preparing an area to reflect the setting of a book. In some classrooms, the level of teacher involvement and direction for role-play is even greater. Morado, Koenig and Wilson (1999) report on their work with children from reception to year two in which they brought together 'literature, drama, music and movement' (p116). The children developed miniperformances that drew on an initial reading of a story. The teachers guided the process through six 30-minute sessions over three weeks. The more formal role-play entailed creating a script using the children's own words, the children's use of these scripts, and the performance given to a small audience of classmates, teachers and family. Through this process, the children heard the story read a number of times, helped to produce the writing of the script, learned the words of the script, and demonstrated their literacy to the family. All this developed from enjoyment of a story.

Drawing and writing

Children enjoy drawing and writing about story characters. In one first year class the teacher chose *Four Fierce Kittens* (Dunbar, 1991) to read to them. Some of the children responded by telling and writing the story themselves. The teacher wrote four of the key words on a word wall: *kittens, frighten, scare,* and *animals.* The children's responses and writing revealed the different levels of confidence with print. One wrote a simple sentence of nine words:

one day fore kittens went to scare the sheep.

The sentence does not begin with a capital letter but does end with a full stop. The child used two of the displayed words, *kittens* and *scare*. In addition, six words are written conventionally. The one invented spelling, *fore*, is an appropriate representation for the word *four*.

Another child wrote rather more (see Figure 12), starting with the fairy tale opening of 'Once upon a time...' There are four sentences, which are each marked by capital letters and full stops, although capital letters appear at other times too. All the words are spelled conventionally.

Both the children's responses include the main feature of the story: it's about kittens scaring other creatures on a farm. However, the author of the second piece was able to extend that idea and also explain the kittens' behaviour.

As the children write their own versions of a story, they may reveal which parts they found most important. For example, *Rosie's Walk* (Hutchins, 1987) has a hen as the main character, a fox appears only in the illustrations but no reference is made to it in the text. Five-year-old John wrote a version including the fox in his retelling, and remarked in his final sentence that he enjoyed the story because the bag of flour fell on the fox (Figure 13).

Intriguingly, John was confident enough to use *decided, sneaked* and *stalking* in his writing. Other children will be far more constrained in their writing, although they may make fewer reversals and have clearer handwriting than John.

If Rosie the hen can go for a walk, then so can the teacher and young children. This extends the story and leads to other writing activities. John's class went for a walk, talking with the adults about what they were seeing as they walked. When they returned to the

Figure 12: Four sentences about kittens

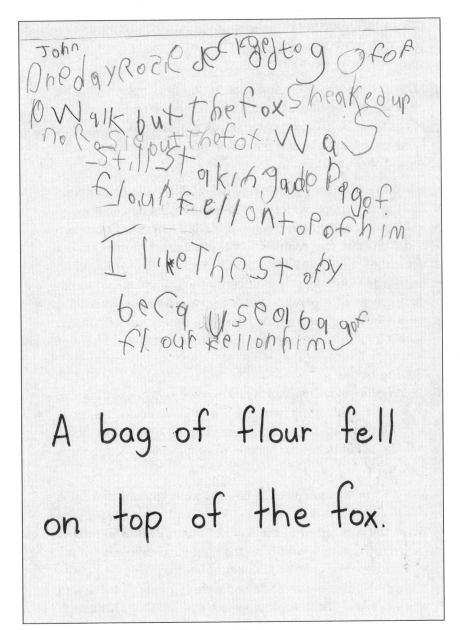

John

One day Rosie ...... to go for
O walk but the fox sneaked up
no Rosie but the fox was
still taking ... bag of
flour fell ontop of him
I like the story
be... use a bag of
flour fell on him

A bag of flour fell

on top of the fox.

Figure 13: John's version of *Rosie's Walk*

classroom, the teacher gave them the opportunity to represent the walk with words and pictures. Michael wrote about what he had seen (see Figure 14).

Michael's writing is characterised by his imagination and his observation. The rabbits may have been hopping on the grass, but Michael was thinking beyond that when he suggested they were looking for carrots. We can only guess at why graves appear as his second observation.

It is not just younger primary school children who benefit from hearing exciting stories read to them and having time to respond to them through writing. Nicholson (2006) describes how year 5 and 6 children had complex stories read aloud to them, talked about those books, reread them in various ways (see Chapter 6), used drama and role play and then wrote about them. The children appeared to develop a wider understanding of their own writing by engaging with the texts. All primary school children benefit from story readings that foster their writing.

Making books

Children love to be involved in making their own books. They can do so in a small group, with the whole class, or on their own. According to Burman (1990), both class and individual book-making should be regular features of young children's classroom experience.

Michael wrote a short piece on his own, while knowing that it was also to contribute to a class book. The class book was titled *Our Walk*, and was linked to the story of *Rosie's Walk*. The teacher pasted the children's writing on the right-hand pages and neatly summarised their contributions on the left-hand pages. Opposite Michael's writing, she wrote, 'We went past the church. In the yard we saw graves.' The clear print on each left-hand page helped the children read the book for themselves. They could recognise that the teacher had used their words. The book was placed in the

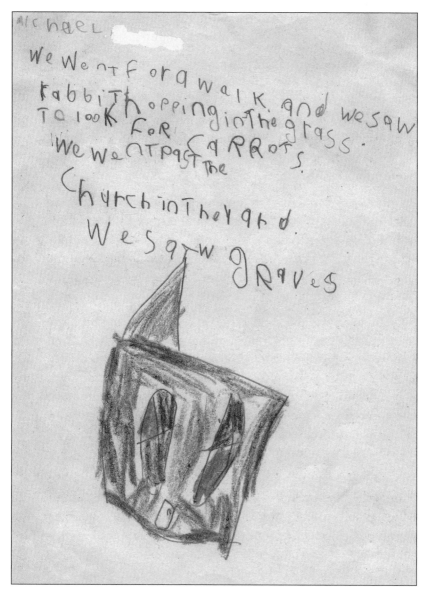

Michael,

We went for a walk. and we saw
rabbit hopping in the grass.
To look for carrots.
We went past the
church in the yard.
We saw graves

Figure 14: Michael's writing after class walk

classroom library and the children felt they had authored *Our Walk* and took pride in the sense of ownership.

On another occasion the children might contribute to a class book as part of a shared or interactive writing session as they re-create a story (see Chapter 7). Again, this allows children to feel that they have authored the book. The individual contributions of each child will be less evident in the finished product of a shared writing. However their efforts from an interactive writing session will be clear for all to see.

By producing class books in these ways, children complete the circle of reading, writing and reading. The story reading excites their interest and provides a basis for creating their own writing. Their writing forms a book for them and others to read. And the collaborative texts help build a library of treasured books in the class.

In addition to class books, children also enjoy making books by themselves. Burman (1990) suggests that one way to help children start writing is to ask what they know a lot about. From this discussion, the teacher can help the children create a brainstorming web that provides a plan for the writing. The class can also create a web about a book from a read-aloud session. Each child can then draw and write about characters or other features of the book, recreate the story or develop another one.

There are several ways to help children create individual books. For example, the teacher can simply staple together the children's drawings and writing. Alternately, each child can write in an eight page booklet – what Johnson (1998) calls an 'origami book' (p9). It consists of front and back covers and three double spreads inside, making six pages. This, Johnson argues, is an ideal writing project planner. When the six pages are seen as three spreads, he writes, the 'fundamental story structure of beginning, middle and end fits it like a glove' (p8).

Children take pleasure in making and using these little books. They can see immediately that the task is manageable and that when they are done they will have made their own book. I have seen children enjoying authoring their own little books from the nursery classroom right through to year 6. As Routman observes, the books become 'a fantastic and favourite resource' (1991, p90). The attraction of being an author and having ownership of a book they have made encourages children to draw and write about the stories they enjoy in read-alouds.

Arts and crafts

When children use a booklet to re-create their response to a story, they usually put in some drawings. In the eight page format they typically enjoy creating a picture on each page, followed by a word, phrase or sentence of description. Thus they are already linking art to literacy as a follow-up to hearing a story read.

Children also enjoy creating larger pictures of the key characters or events in the story. When the classroom is organised so that children can paint at various times throughout the day, many children paint in response to a story reading. Morrow (1989) suggests that reception classrooms should be set up to include an art centre. Hart-Hewins and Wells (1999) also mention having a separate paint centre, even if space allows for only one specialised centre. A selection of paints and paper are the tools for the children to explore their interest in the story.

The teacher can use the children's enthusiasm for representing aspects of the story in paint. Many early years teachers create opportunities for children to create a collage of events from a story. This activity encourages the children to paint, work collaboratively and discuss the best organisation for the collage. Cloth, cardboard, foil, tissue paper and other materials can be stuck onto a three-dimensional collage. The children remain engrossed in the details of the story, which character to paint, which events to depict, so that while they are painting, the children are also developing their skills in literacy.

Once the collage is completed and on display, the class can discuss what print to include. For instance, if the collage is about *The Very Hungry Caterpillar*, they might choose to write some of the words, phrases and sentences from the story. Producing this writing for the collage provides further opportunities for the teacher and children to work together on literacy. We saw in Chapter 1 how a reception class worked together to add print to their caterpillar collage:

Teacher:	That caterpillar is among all the strawberries. How many strawberries have we got?
Jamie:	Four.
Teacher:	We have. So what shall we write here?
Danny:	On ... On Thursday he eated four strawberries.
Teacher:	He did.
	On Thursday *he ate through* *four strawberries,* *but*
Children:	*he was still* *hungry.*
Teacher:	So I'll write *On*. Who is going to help me?
Teresa:	*O* and *n*.
Teacher:	That's right: *On*.

This short excerpt shows how the children were involved in producing writing as they returned to the enjoyment of the story. We can notice, too, how the teacher accepted Danny's contribution and immediately provided a model of the actual words from the book. All the children know that 'he was still hungry.' And Teresa was able to help the teacher write the first word: *On*. From time to time the class returned to the completed collage for shared reading, an extension of reading stories in which the entire class can see the text and focus on print features (for more on shared reading see Chapter 7).

Children also enjoy constructing models as part of their response to a story. Boxes and other scrap material are useful. So are paper, glue, scissors, boxes, egg cartons, toothpicks, cotton balls and other materials. Dough or clay are also good. Each opportunity to construct a model can extend the children's thinking about the story. Pahl (1999) argues that for some children, especially boys, model making is an important link to literacy. She was looking at the pre-school classroom, but she also notes how a child in year two became very involved in writing when this activity was related to a model he had just constructed. Many children are thinking of a narrative and developing their understanding of a text, as they paint and construct.

Making and using puppets

Making puppets is another way of linking with a specific story. The reception class featured in Chapter 1 used stick puppets as part of a reading of *The Very Hungry Caterpillar*. This generated so much interest that the children later decided to make mouse puppets, after the teacher read them another book by Carle, *Do You Want to Be My Friend?* (1991).

Powell and Hornsby (1998) describe how three children in a year two class created stick puppets after they heard a reading of *Possum Magic* (Fox, 1983). They used the puppets as part of their own play activities, and wrote a script for their puppet play. Younger children too can plan a puppet play, and a few may be able to begin to construct a simple script.

One of the attractions of stick puppets is that they are easy to make. The child draws a picture of the character, cuts it out and attaches it to a handle made of a stick or rolled paper. Objects from the story or features of its setting, such as four strawberries, can be drawn, cut out and attached to a handle to become part of the story to be told by the young puppeteers.

Or children might create glove or finger puppets, or masks. Some shy children become more vocal when the glove, finger or mask is the main object of attention. And as the children act out or re-create the story, its words and rhythms remain in their thinking and are remembered.

Songs and rhymes

Children enjoy singing songs and rhymes that relate to the subject of a book, and the activity increases their learning. Ruby Campbell (1998) relates how a story can inspire a wide variety of learning. In a pre-school classroom, the teacher read *Barn on Fire* (Amery, 1989). What appears in the story to be a fire in a barn is actually smoke from a picnic fire on the other side of the barn. The teacher then sang the following song:

> *London's burning,*
> *London's burning.*
> *Fetch the engine,*
> *Fetch the engine.*
> *Fire, Fire,*
> *Fire, Fire.*
> *Pour on water,*
> *Pour on water.*

The class went on to learn the song, together with actions such as holding a hand to the mouth to call out 'Fire, Fire' and pretending to 'pour on water' with an imaginary bucket. The children were at first puzzled about why they would use a bucket to pour on water so the teacher explained:

My song is about London a long time ago when the houses were made of wood and they were very close together. There were no telephones

88

to get fire engines and they had to use buckets to 'pour on water.' Shall we sing it again?

> *London's burning,*
> *London's burning* ... (Campbell, 1998, p134)

At the end of the school day, the children were to be seen telling the adults who had come to collect them all about the story, or singing the song to them.

This link with parents is important to ensure that some of the literacy learning in the classroom is further developed at home (Weinberger, Hannon, and Nutbrown, 1990). Some pre-schools and schools give out a list of the days when parents are encouraged to visit the classroom and work alongside the children. Such visits enable parents to witness a story reading. Or the story reading may be demonstrated and debated during parent-teacher meetings. The link enables the parents to share some of the children's excitement of the learning that takes place during and following a reading. And it means that when children continue singing and taking part in other activities at home, long after the story reading has taken place, their parents can enhance their learning.

Reading stories leads into other reading activities. Some of the many possibilities are explored in the next chapter.

7

Interactive reading activities

Shared reading

In *The Foundations of Literacy*, Don Holdaway (1979) introduced and developed the important activity of 'shared book experience'. In recent years this has become known as 'shared
reading' (Smith and Elley, 1994), but the nature of the activity
remains the same. The adult demonstrates the reading process
with a Big Book or other large print, and the children contribute to
the activity by reading some of the print, making comments and
asking questions. Such literacy activity is used widely in classrooms with young children – and for good reason.

There is an important difference between reading stories with
young children and shared reading, which is to do with the visibi-
lity of the print. The print used for a shared reading is large – to be
'seen, shared and discussed' (Holdaway, 1979, p64). The book may
be held or placed on a stand. Teachers place themselves in a position that does not obscure the children's view.

During shared reading, the teacher is likely to talk about the print
more and to draw from the children's comments and questions
about the text. This replicates the one-on-one read-aloud ex-

perience the children may have at home, when they can see the print easily. In addition, shared reading provides additional opportunities for the class to discuss characters, events and story meanings.

Holdaway (1979) describes an example of a shared reading as it was first developed He reports on the reading and the questions the teacher asks. The blanks indicate where the children joined in.

Teacher: *One day she met a frog.*   'Who is she talking to?'
         She said – - —:   'How many words?'
         'Frog, frog,
         please play with me   A repetitive section suitable
         I'm all by myself   for chiming in.
         As you can see.'

         'Yes,' said the frog,
         'I will — — —,   'What does she want him to do?'

         We will play at j—.   'Perhaps discuss names beginning with *j*.

(Holdaway, 1979, p69)

This account shows how the teacher encourages thinking about the text and the print. For instance, just as in a story reading, the children are encouraged to join in with the repetitive section of the story. Then the teacher's question 'What does she want him to do?' prompts the children to consider the events of the story. The teacher may also use the story's letters and letter sounds to link the word *jumping* with children's names beginning with *j*. This helps them consider letters and sounds within the context of the story.

Slaughter (1992) also examines shared book experiences. Like Holdaway, she argues that the use of Big Books enables the classroom teacher to 'simulate the bedtime story experience' (p16). Slaughter suggests a range of activities that could follow from reading the story, and indicates a number of simple but valuable practical points for the classroom teacher to note.

Teachers should use the same criteria for selecting books for shared reading as they do for story reading. The stories should have the familiar features of repetition, rhyme and rhythm (Rhodes, 1981). In some instances, a particularly appropriate book that fosters predictability may not be available in Big Book format so the teacher may decide to create a Big Book from the text. Other material may be produced in large format for the purpose of shared reading, such as nursery rhymes, songs, poems and notices.

Shared reading also gives teachers an opportunity to read from various non-fiction texts, including dictionaries (Goodwin and Redfern, 2000). As teachers read passages from science and social science texts, they can draw pupils' attention to the use of layout, headings, numbered sections, bold print, contents, index and glossary. Such discussions help young children understand the differences between narrative and informative texts. This under-standing assists the children's own reading and writing of different genres.

The teacher in one reception class selected the Big Book of *Rosie's Walk* (Hutchins, 1987) for shared reading. During the first reading, the emphasis was on the sheer enjoyment of the text. Never-theless, the teacher followed the print with a pointer as she read. During the second reading, she talked about some of this print:

Teacher: Can you remember what this first page says?

             Rosie the

Children: *hen went for a walk*

Teacher: Yes. *Rosie the hen went for a walk.* So where does it say *hen*? You come and show me, Brian.

             [Brian points to the word hen with the pointer.]

Teacher: Yes, that's right. How many letters are there in *hen*?

Anna:	Three.
Teacher:	Yes, that's right. What are the letters?
Tina:	*h-e-n.*
Teacher:	Yes, *h-e-n.*

Later in this shared reading, the children commented on the other main character in the story:

Sam:	It doesn't say *fox* anywhere.
Teacher:	No, it doesn't, but we know the fox is in the story don't we?
Michelle:	We can see the picture.
Teacher:	Yes, that's right, the fox is always there. What is the first letter for *fox*?
Sam:	*f*
Teacher:	Yes, the letter *f.*
Jane:	And it's got an *x.*
Teacher:	It has, but there is another letter in between. I'll write *f* and *x*, but what else do we need for *fox*? [She places an emphasis on the *o*.]

Engaging the children thus, the teacher continued talking about the three letters in *fox*. This excerpt shows how the enjoyment of the story was followed by a consideration of the words used about the two main characters. Even though the word *fox* is not written in the text, it became significant.

Slaughter's (1992) also writes about work on *Rosie's Walk* with a first year class. After the teacher read the story, the class spent a week engaged in a various activities based on the text. The letters *R* and *H* became a major focus of the print. On the Tuesday, a group of children looked through the book in search of words beginning with *R* or *H*. Then they identified the children in the class whose names started with these letters. The class worked on charts of words that begin with *R* or *H*. In addition to those words they found in *Rosie's Walk*, the children added others. In all, they produced eleven words for each letter. They followed the story by writing, making puppets, and listening to other stories by Pat Hutchins.

Teachers do not have to choose between story reading and shared reading. Both have a part in children's literacy development. The daily story reading is about the story and sometimes the activities that flow naturally from it and from the children's interest in it. The shared reading allows for closer consideration of the print, although many additional activities can flow from the reading. But the enjoyment of the text is in all cases paramount. As Brenda Parkes (2000) notes, 'the first purpose of shared reading is to pro-vide children with an enjoyable reading experience' (p1). The nature of literacy activities must not be allowed to become so analytical that the children lose interest in the stories, books and reading.

Sustained silent reading

Sustained Silent Reading (SSR) is a natural activity that gives sup-port to story readings. When young children are given a chance to engage in SSR, they can act out reading-like behaviours. And they have the opportunity to read a well-loved book on their own, using the model that has been provided by the adult through numerous story readings and shared readings. Not every child will read silently. The youngest will vocalise as they read, and some children will comment on a picture or the relationship of the story to their own life. But each child is moving toward silent reading.

Other acronyms have been used to describe SSR such as Sustained Quiet Un-Interrupted Reading Time (SQUIRT) and Drop Every-thing and Read (DEAR). In one year 1 classroom, the children had an allocated time for BE A Reader (BEAR). Capitalising on the acronym the teacher encouraged an exploration of books about bears. Pictures, models, toys, and the children's own writing about Winnie the Pooh, Paddington, Big Bear, Little Bear and other bears added to the children's excitement and interest.

Typically, teachers use a short period for SSR every day. For ease of organisation, this is usually just before or after a break. Trelease (1995) describes a classroom where the children selected a book before they went to lunch and left it on their desk ready for SSR time in the ten minutes after lunch. This short period of silent reading adds up to almost an hour of concentrated reading each week.

The children select their own books during this reading period and are not required to report on what they read. Trelease (1995) stresses that adults in the room must also read during this time, as this gives children a strong model of reading. Hart-Hewins and Wells (1990), however, suggest that the teacher may want to use SSR as a time to hold individual reading conferences. Considering the differing views, Campbell and Scrivens (1995) note that the best course of action will be determined by the overall ethos of the classroom. In classrooms where there is a dynamic literacy pro-gramme operating, with an enthusiastic teacher who supports literacy activities, modelling during SSR is not essential. When there is less emphasis on literacy, modelling appears to be re-quired to keep the children reading. The real issue may be to en-sure that SSR is organised so that the young children are aware of the nature and importance of this worthwhile activity.

Individual reading
The individual reading activity can be viewed in a number of ways. First, it might be seen as a one-to-one interaction where the adult reads to the child. This type of interaction is especially important for children who have not had experiences of story readings before they began school and even though they have daily story readings and shared reading in the classroom. Individual story readings allow the teacher or other adults to ensure that the child is

involved and is contributing to the story and beginning to pick up on print features.

Alternatively, the individual reading activity can be used for individual reading conferences. It is the child who reads to the teacher during these conferences, especially in the later years of primary school. Holdaway (1979) maintains that the shared book experience fosters individual reading as the child rereads a book they have heard read by the teacher. After the reading, adult and child can discuss the content of the text and discuss various aspects of print.

To see how this works, I studied 6-year-old Leah's individual reading of *Good-Night Owl* (Hutchins, 1972) with her Year 1 teacher (Campbell, 1990, p47-53). In the following transcript, the original text appears in parentheses after her miscues:

Leah:	*The starlings chittered,*
	tweet-tweet (twit-twit) tweet-tweet (twit-twit)
	and owl tried to sleep.
	The jays screamed,
	ark ark,
	and owl tried to sleep.
	The cuckoo croaked (called)
Teacher:	*The cuckoo*
Leah:	*called*

Leah could read a good deal of this book, partly because she remembered the text and partly because she paid attention to the print. The teacher had to determine when to mediate in the reading. She ignored the miscue of *tweet-tweet* (*twit-twit*), but she did support Leah's reading when the child read *croaked* for *called*. Using the simple strategy of starting the sentence again, the teacher gave Leah time to reflect, to consider the word in context, and to self-correct.

Later, once the whole book had been read, the teacher developed a dialogue with Leah that emphasised meaning:

Teacher:	Why couldn't he sleep?
Leah:	Because they were all making a noise.
Teacher:	Why do you think they were all making a noise? Mmh?
Leah:	Because it's still-umh...
Teacher:	In when?
Leah:	Because it's not night yet.
Teacher:	It isn't night time. And what do owls do at night time?
Leah:	They – They don't – umh – They don't sleep in night and they wake up....

It was evident that Leah knew about the story even though she was hesitant in some of her attempts to explain. With support from the teacher she was able to sustain her involvement with the text throughout the individual reading. Individual reading activities build children's confidence and enable them to behave like readers.

Buddy reading

The everyday demands of the classroom limit the time the teacher and other adults can spend working alongside a young child with a book. Consequently, some schools have initiated schemes such as buddy reading (Cunningham and Allington, 1999) and pairing a year four or five reader with a younger child. Once a week, the older child goes to read a book with the younger child.

Buddy reading has a number of benefits. First, the older children must practice reading the picture book to ensure that it is read well for the younger ones. For some 9- and 10-year-olds, that practice can be important. As Cunningham and Allington indicate, it 'legitimises the reading and rereading of very easy books' (p38). Further, the important teaching role helps the older children with their own reading development, and does much for their self-esteem. At the same time, the younger buddies benefit from the interactive experience of the story reading.

In addition, the buddy system gives the younger children positive role models. In particular, young boys may benefit from the presence of successful boy readers, especially as most early years classrooms are staffed by women. As Cunningham and Allington remind us, 'most elementary teachers are women and...most poor readers are boys' (p37). Some schools extend buddy reading to include adults from the community.

As the front cover of this book shows, buddy reading also occurs naturally in a home setting. The secondary aged child in the picture is reading to a nursery child, who is utterly involved. During the reading a primary aged child was attracted by the story and became part of the audience. When young children know how interesting stories can be, they are on the lookout for someone of whatever age to read to them.

Paired reading

In addition to buddy reading, classmates can work together to read a book. So paired reading (or partner reading) can operate with two 5-year-old reception children or two 6-year-old Year 1 children helping each other to read a book. Cunningham and Allington (1999) suggest that the teacher designate a number of different activities to create some variety for paired reading:

> During a 'take turn day,' the two children read alternate pages. They also help each other as the need arises. This is likely to be the most frequently used form of paired reading; the children soon become familiar with the approach and are able to use it successfully.

> An 'ask question day' requires both children to read each page silently and ask each other a question about the text before proceeding. In some first- and second-year classrooms, the teacher may encourage the children to ask questions about features of the print on one day and to encourage a greater attention to the story content on another day.

Another day might be used as a 'sticky note day.' The teacher gives the children a limited number of sticky notes to mark what interests them. Alternately, the children can concentrate on what they consider to be important or aspects they find confusing.

A 'you decide day' permits the children to make their own decision as to how they will operate the paired reading on that day.

As Cunningham and Allington note, these different forms of paired reading create variety, encourage the children to engage in both silent and oral reading, and lead them to reflect on what they have read.

Guided reading

In a typical guided reading time, the teacher works with a small group of children. Six is the ideal size for a group. Each child has a copy of a book they can manage and enjoy. For younger children, their management of the text is supported when the book has already been read aloud to the class. The purpose of guided reading is to 'develop independent readers who question, consider alternatives, and make informed choices as they seek meaning' (Mooney, 1990, p47). She sees the teacher's role as being to guide the children to predict as they read, to sample features of print, to confirm that meaning has been maintained, and to self-correct using other strategies to regain meaning.

The teacher then guides the children with their reading of a certain book, but does so in ways that will help the children to read other texts independently in the future. Fountas and Pinnell (1996) provide detailed information on this activity. Chomsky-Higgins (1998) suggests the choice of a book that the children can read successfully but that does offer some challenges. If the book is new to the children she tells them the title, and together they go through the book to get an idea of its meaning and she asks the children to read certain specific words. After this supportive introduction, the children read the book aloud, while she moves around the group to listen in and guide when needed. A brief discussion may follow the reading.

Literature circles

Young children also need reading to help them make sense of life (Short, 1999). Short argues that children should not have to wait until they've developed extended reading strategies to find out that reading involves critique and inquiry. In literature circles, as in guided reading, the teacher works with a small group of children who each have a copy of the same book. During literature circles, however, the primary interest centres on thinking about and discussing the story.

When quality picture books are read aloud, the children want to discuss what they see and hear. They are keen to express their thoughts and feelings about the books that are read to them or that they have read in small groups (Roser and Martinez, 1995). At first the teacher will have to prompt and guide them, but eventually the children will offer their own comments.

The children's participation in literature circles is not surprising: even toddlers at home respond reflectively to stories they hear read aloud. When I read *The Very Lonely Firefly* (Carle, 1995) to my granddaughter Alice when she was 3 years 11 months old she immediately requested a repeat reading. But within a few pages of that second reading, as the lonely firefly searches for other fireflies, Alice interrupted me to remark: 'It will find the other fireflies on the last page. Then it won't be lonely anymore.' The last page, with its illustrations of flashing lights, is a particular attraction of this book. Alice returned to her theme when we reached it. 'There's all its friends' (Campbell, 1999, p89-90). Her comments show Alice's involvement with the story and her empathy for the firefly as it searched for others.

Adults and teachers can encourage children's responses to reading at home and in the classroom as they read aloud with them. And such responses can be developed in literature circles as the children progress through the primary years.

What children learn from story readings provides a strong base for their work during other interactive reading activities. In addition, as Chapter 1 showed, reading stories with young children can also serve as the foundation for interactive writing activities. This subject is examined in Chapter 8.

8

Interactive writing activities

Just as teachers point out print features in Big Books to assist reading, they can write in front of the class to help children become better writers. During shared writing (Cambourne, 1988), the teacher talks about the piece as it's developed, so making the children aware of the writing process. Interactive writing, guided writing and writing conferences also require the children's involvement as they contribute to the writing, or share their own, by considering their thoughts, sentences, words and letters.

Shared writing

The stories, songs, poems and rhymes the children already know are good starting points for shared writing. I observed how a teacher in a pre-school class used the popular nursery rhyme, Humpty Dumpty, to create a brief shared writing time with the children (Campbell, 1996, p51-52). The class had talked about the rhyme and had often sung it. The teacher wrote on a large sheet of paper in front of the children encouraging them to tell her the words:

Teacher: So if I write

Humpty Dumpty

Now, what comes next?

Children: *sat on a wall*

Teacher: I'll write

sat on a...

Children: *wall*

Teacher: *wall.*

There we are.

Humpty Dumpty

Teacher/children: *sat on a wall.*

Teacher: Now

Humpty

Children: *Dumpty*

had a great fall.

This simple example illustrated how the children recited the rhyme and the teacher tried to keep up with their pace. Her goal was to support the children in understanding the writing process and the link between words spoken and words presented in print. She encouraged their contributions by asking questions such as 'Now, what comes next?' and by using rising intonation and pausing such as 'sat on a....'

This shared writing activity sometimes included shared reading. After she wrote down the first sentence, the teacher pointed to the words and recited them with the children. When the rhyme was complete, she put the printed rhyme on the classroom wall beside other rhyme sheets that had been created during shared writing. The class used the sheets all through the year to recite the rhymes while the teacher pointed to the words.

Teachers of reception children usually spend longer considering each word as it is written. They might comment on letters and letter-sounds, and make links between the first letter of some words and of other words the children know.

Geekie, Cambourne, and Fitzsimmons (1999) observe a reception classroom where the teacher followed a structure they describe as follows:

i)   Making a clear statement about what is going to be written.

ii) Identifying each word in succession.

iii) Either

      a.   recalling the identified word from memory

      b.   finding it in the print environment of the classroom and copying it

      c.   segmenting it into phonemes and making sound-symbol matches

iv) Re-reading the developing text in order to remember what has already been written and what remains to be written. (p40)

The teacher used what she called 'blackboard stories': stories developed with the children, to link to other print in the classroom including the word wall. This regular practice enabled the children gradually to write stories on their own.

Anderson (1995) adopted a different strategy in a Year 1 and 2 mixed classroom with 6- and 7-year-old children. To encourage the children to think about choices when writing, she selected a text they knew and loved – *The Very Hungry Caterpillar* – and printed the story in large text for all the children to see. She asked them whether they would have used the same words and phrases as the author had. A great deal of discussion ensued as the children changed aspects of the story. The start of the story became

One dark cloudy night a tiny speckled egg lay on a leaf.
One bright Saturday morning the warm sun came up and – crack! – out

of the egg came a tiny and very hungry caterpillar.
She scrambled about to look for some food.
On Sunday she ate through one nice ripe apple. But she was still hungry.
On Monday she ate through two red shiny apples, but she was still hungry.
On Tuesday she ate through three squidgy plums, but she was still hungry. (p48)

Every redrafting involved discussion, which meant that the children were talking about meaning, sentences, phrases, words and letters. And because it seemed natural to do so, the teacher found herself using terms such as adjective, pronoun, noun and verb. At one point, they even discussed the notion of tense in story writing.

We see that the caterpillar became 'she' rather than 'he.' Starting with a Saturday changed the link between days of the week and events. The class added adjectives to describe each fruit. For a while they played with alliterations, debating the use of 'plump purple plums' before settling for their own word: *squidgy*. The teacher typed up the revised text on the computer put and put it in book format for the class library, where it became one of the most popular books.

Elsewhere, a year 6 class rewrote the picture book story *Giggle, Giggle, Quack* (Cronin, 2002), but changing it so that the story was written from the duck's perspective. As always a reading of the story to the class and discussion preceded the writing. The children's recreation of the story was quite imaginative, as we can see from the way one of the boys in the class rewrote the beginning of the story:

'Hmmm... Farmer Brown is going away and Bob doesn't know a thing about farms. We can do anything we like if we utilise this note system.' Duck walked over to the shed where the other animals were.
'What do you want for dinner?' he shouted.
Twenty-nine minutes later the pizza arrived and all

the animals started to eat. He had left a note for Bob saying
that every Tuesday was pizza night.
'Oh, that Bob is so gullible!' duck laughed.

Well-known stories are a good basis for other shared writing experiences. Johnson and Louis (1985) assert that writing literary letters also creates genuine opportunities for writing. They suggest that children might write their own letters to a character in a familiar story, such as Mike from *Mike Mulligan and His Steam Shovel* (Burton, 1977), and the teacher could reply. In a classroom where *The Very Hungry Caterpillar* has been read, the teacher might choose to reply to a letter such as the one shown in Figure 15, which was written by a Year two child.

In particular, the teacher might wish to pick up on the scientific inquiry which appears in the last sentence: 'How long are you going to stay in your cocoon?'

In an example drawn from work with older primary children, Johnson and Louis suggest that the class could work together to compose such a letter, the teacher leading the discussion with the children and scribing their thoughts. The teacher can emphasise on different features of the writing process to suit what the class needs at the time. The emphasis will be mainly on meaning, but the teacher may also draw the class's attention to the print features of the letters, words, phrases and sentences the children select.

Interactive writing

McCarrier, Pinnell and Fountas (1999) suggest that while shared writing is an important literacy activity for young children, it's possible to involve the children even further in what they call *interactive writing*. Interactive writing proceeds like shared writing, but the children take turns writing the words in front of the class, supported and guided by the teacher. The teacher also writes some of the words as part of that support.

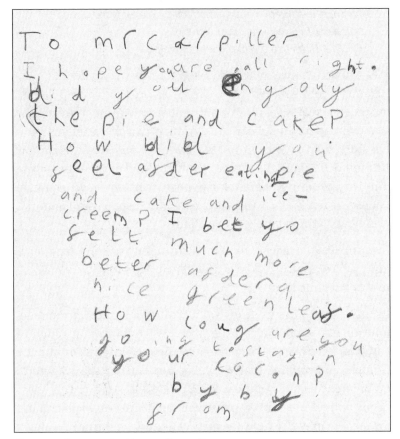

Figure 15: Letter to the Hungry Caterpillar

As these authors point out, 'sharing the pen is not simply a ritual'; instead, there is instructional value every time the child writes with the pen in front of the class (p21). They argue that interactive writing works well for children from a range of linguistic backgrounds and 'for those transitioning into English literacy' (pxvi) because the children are actively engaged in the writing.

They maintain that the primary value of writing activities lies in the process, not the end product. Interactive writing provides an excellent opportunity for teachers to determine the children's learning needs and plan an activity accordingly, whether for the whole class or a small group. In both cases, the conversation about the writing topic is continuous. The teacher should also discuss the composing process, the conventions of writing, and the interesting features of certain words. For example, when the class is working with the Humpty Dumpty rhyme, the teacher might want to make the rime unit of *all*, *wall*, and *fall* a central feature of discussion.

In one of the many examples given by McCarrier, Pinnell and Fountas (1999), the writing was stimulated by a classroom story reading of *Pancakes, Pancakes* (Carle, 1990). The book linked with the class's study of food and nutrition, and Eric Carle was one of the children's favourite authors. During interactive writing, the class produced a list of pancake ingredients, a list of favourite pancake toppings, and a recipe for making pancakes. Each piece of writing required the children to think and talk about writing and also to help in the process as they shared the pen.

Guided writing

In guided writing the teacher also works with a group of, ideally, four to eight children. The time is generally used either as a group shared writing enterprise, in which the teacher and children work collaboratively on a piece of writing or as a mini-lesson, in which the teacher works with a small group of children with similar needs on a particular feature of writing. For example, the group may decide to write a letter to a character in a story, the teacher emphasising both meaning and form. Because the group is small, each child can input more and remain involved. Collaborative writing concentrates on the production of the content, but features of print are also discussed.

Graves (1994) describes the beginning of the writing in one reception classroom:

Teacher: What do I want to say? Let's see.

> 'Billy and I go for walks.'
> Help me.
> B...il...ly (She says the word very slowly)
> Help me with the first sound 'B.'
> What letter do I write here?
>
> Brendan: B. I've got that one in my own name. It's easy. (p49)

This is an example of aspects of print being discussed. Like many children in reception, Brendan can use knowledge of his name to help in producing other writing.

As a mini-lesson, guided writing gives children concentrated time, in a small group, to consider some aspect of writing conventions. The objective of the short lesson may be to think about letters and sounds, punctuation, vocabulary, or spelling. For instance, a teacher working with a small group of Year 1 children wanted to remind them of sentence conventions began by looking at each sentence of a short book and talked about the uppercase letters and punctuation. Then they read a piece of classroom print developed from a shared writing, again concentrating on the uppercase letters and punctuation. Finally, the children moved on to independent writing, and the teacher confirmed that their use of an initial capital letter and sentence ending was correct. Although mini-lessons in guided writing are brief, they can support children's literacy development, especially when directed by the teacher to meet their needs at the time.

Writing conferences

As they respond to stories, children write in a various formats. They might create a drawing accompanied by writing or make their own book. One-on-one writing conferences (Calkins, 1983) are particularly useful if held immediately after the child has finished writing, so this is still at the forefront of the child's mind. Furthermore, focusing on a single aspect of writing enhances understanding of that feature.

In one classroom, the teacher chose *It's My Birthday* (Oxenbury, 1993) for a story reading. The central theme is about making a cake – a number of animals work together to make it. The second page of the book reads:

> *'It's my birthday and*
> *I'm going to make a cake.*
> *I need some eggs.'*
> *'I'll get you some eggs,'*
> *said the chicken.*

After several readings of the story, some children decided to make their own recipe books. Five-year-old Kate wrote about making a fruitcake (see Figure 16). She was clearly in charge of her writing and used several invented spellings and a mixture of uppercase and lowercase letters in her recipe.

After Kate finished writing, she had a writing conference with the teacher. The teacher praised Kate's writing and talked to her about one of the words she had written unconventionally:

Teacher: I think this would make a great fruitcake. You've done well with your writing.

And to finish we have to ... [She points to 6- *Bac in the ovn*]

Kate: Bake in the oven.

Teacher: That's right. When we write *bake* it is *b-a-k-e*. It is just like cake.

Kate: *C-a-k-e*.

Teacher: I know another one that begins with m.

Kate: *Make.*

Teacher: That's right, *make.*

Kate: *M-a-k-e.*

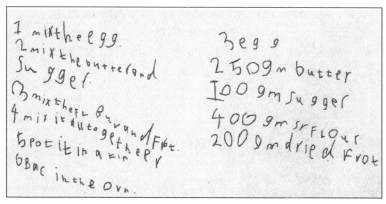

Figure 16: Kate's Fruitcake Recipe

Teacher:	Good girl, that's how to write *make*. Well done, Kate; it's a lovely recipe.
Kate:	*Take* is one as well.
Teacher:	It is, isn't it?

The teacher helped Kate examine the word bake, then they discussed other rime words in the -*ake* family. Interestingly, although the teacher was ready to end the conference, Kate was in full swing and came up with another word: *take*. The conference may have been short, but it was personal so there's a good chance that Kate would recall the -*ake* words in the future and write others like it, such as *lake* and *rake* (Goswami and Bryant, 1990).

Reading stories can lead children into a variety of interactive writing activities. Sometimes the teacher leads the children in certain directions at others the children want to explore further the story they have just heard, such as when the children decided to create recipe books after hearing *It's My Birthday*. The next chapter discusses other directions in which story reading might take.

9

Mathematics, science and social studies activities

Some stories bring other curriculum areas to the children's attention as they ask questions related to the story. Their questions may lead to discussions about content relating to mathematics, science and social studies.

Mathematics

In Chapter 2 we saw how *The Very Hungry Caterpillar* led a reception class to explore aspects of mathematics and science. The children encountered the sequence of numbers 1 to 5 as the caterpillar consumed the apple, pears, plums, strawberries and oranges. For most children, the sequence became firmly established, and they began to recognise the quantities of 1 to 5. When drawing pictures of the five fruits labelling them and creating their own list of five other fruits, their understanding of numbers was established more firmly. The children enjoyed drawing other pictures of the caterpillar, especially recapturing the bold face, and their interest led to other mathematics. The teacher encouraged the children to measure the length of their drawn caterpillar with math cubes. Counting those cubes involved numbers up to 14.

Many storybooks have mathematical features that the teacher can emphasise or follow up as the children begin to talk about them. For instance, in *Hairy Maclary from Donaldson's Dairy* (Dodd, 1983), each dog can be seen coming from its house as they join the pack. The houses are numbered 86, 84 and 82. In one reception classroom, the children noticed these numbers in the illustrations and they wanted to talk about the number on their own houses. Children and teacher asked a numerous questions, such as 'Which is the largest number?' The class then proceeded to create a collage of the 'roads where we live,' painting the numbers on each house. In this instance, the teacher had planned none of these activities; the children's interest set them on the mathematical path. The children were excited by the attention given to the numbers in the story and the numbers on their own houses and they learned from this and from concentrating on 'big numbers'.

A teacher might collect books that are exploring a mathematical theme. For instance, *One Tiger Growls* (Wadsworth, 1999) provides a sequence from 1 to 20 as various animals and their sounds are presented. Accordingly the sequence of 1 to 20 can be learned, or consolidated with an enjoyable story reading. Shatzer (2008) demonstrates how she used *The Wolf's Chicken Stew* (Kasza, 1996) to develop some mathematical themes with her pupils, and list other books she has found helpful in linking literacy and mathematics.

Science

In the reception classroom presented in Chapter 2, the children explored aspects of science after hearing *The Very Hungry Caterpillar.* The life cycle of the butterfly became part of their knowledge base simply from the rereading of the story plus a song about it. Importantly, as the children sang the song, they recognised that the life cycle could 'go on forever'. The story also generated interest in what other animals eat. Then the class explored which foods are nutritious and which are not. It is not difficult to see how *The Very*

Hungry Caterpillar led to thinking about such matters and thus about aspects of science.

In *Sniff-Snuff-Snap!* (Dodd, 1995) the story of the animals and the water hole creates scientific interests for young children. The sequence or cycle of rain and evaporation are part of the story, and this intrigues children. So does the role of the animals that are sustained by the water from the water hole in the otherwise arid land. This generates questions about not only the water supply but also their own water supply. Knowing about a wide range of children's books enables primary school teachers to make connections from stories into science.

Social studies

A story like *Sniff-Snuff-Snap!* can also take children into other areas of the curriculum. What is it like in a country such as the one shown in this story? Discussions about desert lands often arise from stories such as *Sniff-Snuff-Snap!* An interest in geography may start from other stories, too. *Possum Magic* (Fox, 1983) contains a map of Australia that indicates the route taken by the two possums. The possums' journey and the 'people food' they eat capture the attention, feelings and minds of young children, and many want to learn more about Australia, the animals that live there and the foods mentioned. Creating a collage of the unique animals of Australia is an obvious follow-up to hearing this story as the possum, koala, wombat, kangaroo and duck-billed platypus all intrigue young children. Mem Fox's other books such as *Koala Lou* (1988) and *Wombat Divine* (1995) add to the children's knowledge and, most important, are stories they will love.

There are no maps in the story of *Rosie's Walk* (Hutchins, 1987), but Rosie creates a trail that can be mapped by children as they follow her path through the farmyard. A wall collage of Rosie's journey helps young children envision the story and begin to understand the nature of maps. When the children are captivated by the story, the teacher may decide to take them on walks in the local environment and then create maps of that walk. Creating a map of their route to school is another possibility. In this case the geography is local, helping children understand their own environment.

The simple story of *When I Was Little Like You* (Walsh, 1997) also links to other curriculum areas. Here a little girl named Rosie talks with her grandmother and shows her various sights such as a train and an ice-cream van. In each instance, the grandmother observes that 'When I was little like you it used to be different,' and tells her how things used to be when she was young. The historical changes over two generations are the most important features of the story, although relationships are also significant. The story captures the children's interest in how life used to be long ago, and stimulates an interest in history. Often, the class can link this story to family and community history. It inspires children to explore how things used to be when their parents were young.

Stories can be a useful means of introducing young children to history. Hoodless (1998) devotes a complete book to history and English in the primary years, exploring the numerous connections that can be made. The children might also link a classroom story to a theme that is already being pursued: in a case study of reception children in England, Hoodless reports how after enjoying *The Three Billy Goats Gruff*, the children made a connection with an existing theme on Sir Robert Peel and the police. They decided to use the role-play area, which was already arranged as a Victorian police station, to create and hang 'wanted' posters of the troll.

Wendy Hood (1994) shows how one teacher worked with a class of Year 3 children from diverse ethnic backgrounds to link story readings and social studies themes. The children began by trying to find information about Native Americans. Their research over a period of weeks led them in a various directions. They pursued such questions as 'Where did they live? Where do they live now? What holidays do they celebrate?' Their findings also raised questions about slavery. So to develop their understanding, the teacher read certain non-fiction texts aloud to help them extend their knowledge of the theme. At the same time, they also learned more about the organisation of non-fiction books.

This chapter has shown how just a few storybooks have been used to demonstrate the links that can be made between story readings or shared readings and other curriculum areas. However, any resourceful teacher of young children could easily build a repertoire of books with links across the curriculum. Slaughter (1993) suggests a number of titles that can lead into mathematics, science, and social studies or to art and music. Rodgers, Hawthorne and Wheeler (2007) have a list of books that might be read to teach economics to primary children. Such demonstrate that storybooks have the basis to provide interesting support for teaching just about anything.

Children's learning is enhanced when they are given time to explore various topics and interests and their explorations lead to more reading and writing. The teacher will nevertheless want to ensure that the stories are being read for their intrinsic value and the pleasure they give the children. This book ends with a last look at the important part the story reading itself plays in young children's literacy development.

10

A last word

Story readings are enjoyable and instructive. Every teacher of young children can name a story with which they have particularly captivated children. In one classroom, the children particularly enjoyed *Hairy Maclary from Donaldson's Dairy* (Dodd, 1983). The main characters are all dogs. Among them are:

> Hercules Morse
> as big as a horse
> and Hairy Maclary
> from Donaldson's dairy.

As the dogs' adventure unfolded, the children's excitement persisted, and when the reading was over, more than one child asked for it to be read again. Because the characters are so loveable, young children want to return again and again to the story. And the children learn more from each reading.

Luckily for the children, there are several stories about Hairy Maclary (e.g. Dodd, 1985a, 1985b) and other central characters for children to enjoy. Children who are familiar with Hairy Maclary and his friends become excited when the characters unexpectedly reappear in *Slinky Malinki, open the door* (Dodd, 1993). In one infant classroom, the 5-year-olds became involved in a form of author study as they listened to, discussed, commented on and followed the many rhyming books by this author. And there are numerous other authors who have produced stories and characters that capture children's attention. We noted earlier the rhyme in *Fix-It-Duck* (Alborough, 2001)

A leak in the roof.
Oh, what bad luck!
This is a job for...
Fix-It Duck.

and how it encouraged one child's involvement and love of Duck, Sheep, Goat and Frog in this and other Duck books. *Koala Lou* (Fox, 1988) and *The Gruffalo* (Donaldson, 1999) are among the many picture books which lead children eventually into reading chapter books.

The enjoyment children receive from story readings sparks their desire to read for themselves in a way that no worksheet can ever emulate. The thousands of delightful books available for reading aloud provide the foundation for literacy learning. Guided by the story, the children follow their interests by drawing, writing, painting, making puppets, acting, reciting and moving on to areas of the curriculum. Moreover, children develop their phonic knowledge from the meaningful contexts of story readings (Campbell, 2004).

The characters from stories have a way of reappearing as part of children's imaginative play. Chambers (1995) gives a vivid account of a little girl who found a way to walk alone along a poorly lit path by imagining that she was escorted by Little Red Riding Hood. The characters from children's stories become the children's friends. And words, phrases and sentences transfer from the stories into their own lexicon.

Each chapter in this book has emphasised the literacy learning which can follow from the well prepared and enthusiastic reading of a story. Little wonder that so many teachers recognise the benefits of *Reading stories with young* children and ensure that it is an important part of every day.

References

Adams, M.J (1990) *Beginning to read: Thinking and learning about print.* Cambridge, MA: MIT Press

Anderson, H (1995) About as big as the library: Using quality texts in the development of children as readers and writers. In E. Bearne (Ed.) *Great expectations.* London: Cassell

Ashton-Warner, S (1963) *Teacher.* London: Secker and Warburg

Baghban, M (1984) *Our daughter learns to read and write.* Newark, DE: International Reading Association

Bettleheim, B and Zelan, K (1981) *On learning to read.* London: Penguin

Bissex, G (1980) *GNYS AT WRK: A child learns to read and write.* Cambridge, MA: Harvard University Press

booktrustchilrensbooks.org.uk (as accessed September 2008)

Bruner, J (1968) Two modes of thought. In J. Mercer (Ed.) *Language and literacy from an educational perspective.* Vol. I Milton Keynes, UK: Open University Press

Burman, C (1990) Organizing for reading 3-7. In B. Wade (Ed.) *Reading for real.* Buckingham, UK: Open University Press

Butler, D (1998) *Babies need books: Sharing the joy of books with children from birth to six* (Rev. ed.). Portsmouth, NH: Heinemann

Calkins, L (1983) *Lessons from a child: On the teaching and learning of writing.* Portsmouth, NH: Heinemann

Cambourne, B (1988) *The whole story: Natural learning and the acquisition of literacy in the classroom.* Sydney, Australia: Ashton Scholastic

Campbell, R (1990) *Reading together.* Buckingham, UK: Open University Press

Campbell, R (1992) *Reading real books.* Buckingham, UK: Open University Press

Campbell, R (1996) *Literacy in nursery education.* Stoke-on-Trent, UK: Trentham Books

Campbell, R (1999) *Literacy from home to school: Reading with Alice.* Stoke-on-Trent, UK: Trentham

Campbell, R (2001) *Read-Alouds with Young Children.* Newark, DE: International Reading Association

Campbell, R (2004) *Phonics, Naturally: Reading and Writing for Real Purposes.* Portsmouth, NH: Heinemann

Campbell, R.E (1998) A day of literacy learning in a nursery classroom. In R. Campbell (Ed.), *Facilitating preschool literacy* Newark, DE: International Reading Association

Campbell, R and Scrivens, G (1995) The teacher role during Sustained Silent Reading. *Reading,* 29(2) 2-4

Carter, J (1999) The power and the story. *Reading,* 33(2) 87-90

Chambers, A (1995) *Book talk: Occasional writing on literature and children.* Stroud, UK: The Thimble Press

Chomsky-Higgins, P (1998) Teaching strategies and skills during readers' workshop: Setting the stage for successful readers and writers. In C. Weaver (Ed.) *Practicing what we know: Informed reading instruction.* Urbana, IL: National Council of Teachers of English

Chukovsky, K (1963) *From two to five.* Berkeley, CA: University of California Press

Collins, F and Svensson, C (2008) If I had a magic wand I'd magic her out of the book: the rich literacy practices of competent early readers. *Early Years* 28 (1) p81-91

Cullinan, B.E (1989) Literature for young children. In D.S. Strickland and L.M. Morrow (Eds.), *Emerging literacy: Young children learn to read and write.* Newark, DE: International Reading Association

Cunningham, P.M and Allington, R.L (1998) *Classrooms that work: They can all read and write* (2nd ed.). New York: Longman

Doake, D (1988) *Reading begins at birth.* Richmond Hill, ON: Scholastic

Dombey, H (1988) Partners in the telling. In M. Meek and C. Mills (Eds.) *Language and literacy in the primary school.* Lewes, UK: Falmer

Duursma, E, Augustyn, M and Zuckerman, B (2008) *Reading aloud to children: the evidence.* Archives of Disease in Childhood

Elley, W (1989) Vocabulary acquisition from listening to stories. *Reading Research Quarterly,* 24 p176-186

Ericson, L and Juliebö, M.F (1998) *The phonological awareness handbook for kindergarten and primary teachers*. Newark, DE: International Reading Association

Evans, J (1998, October/November) Perfect circles. *Literacy and Learning*, 16-19

Feitelson, D, Kita, B and Goldstein, Z (1986) Effects of listening to series stories on first graders' comprehension and use of language. *Research in the Teaching of English*, 20 p339-356

Fountas, I.C and Pinnell, G.S (1996) *Guided reading: Good first teaching for all children*. Portsmouth, NH: Heinemann

Fox, C (1993) *At the very edge of the forest: The influence of literature on storytelling by children*. London: Cassell

Fox, M (2001) *Reading Magic: Why reading aloud to our children will change their lives forever*. Orlando, USA: Harcourt

Fox, M at www.memfox.net. (as accessed July 2008)

Geekie, P *et al* (1999) *Understanding literacy development*. Stoke-on-Trent, UK: Trentham

Giorgis, C and Johnson, N (1999) Children's books: Reading aloud. *The Reading Teacher*, 53 p80-87

Goddard, N (1958) *Reading in the modern infants' school*. London: University of London Press

Goodman, Y.M (Ed.) (1990) *How children construct literacy: Piagetian perspectives*. Newark, DE: International Reading Association

Goodwin, P and Redfern, A (2000) *Non-fiction in the literacy hour*. Reading, Berkshire, UK: Reading and Language Information Centre

Goswami, U (1999) Causal connections in beginning reading: The importance of rhyme. *Journal of Research in Reading*, 22(3) p217-240

Goswami, U.C. and Bryant, P (1990) *Phonological skills and learning to read*. Hove, UK: Erlbaum

Graham, J. and Kelly, A (1997) *Reading under control: Teaching reading in the primary school*. London: David Fulton

Graves, D.H (1994) *A fresh look at writing*. Portsmouth, NH: Heinemann

Hall, N. and Robinson, A (1985) *Looking at literacy: Using images of literacy to explore the world of reading and writing*. London: David Fulton

Hart-Hewins, L. and Wells, J (1990) *Real books for reading: Learning to read with children's literature*. Portsmouth, NH: Heinemann

Hart-Hewins, L. and Wells, J (1999) *Better books! Better readers*. Markham, ON: Pembroke

Heath, S.B (1982) What no bedtime stories means: Narrative skills at home and school. *Language and Society,* 11 p49-76

Heath, S.B (1983) *Ways with words: Language, life and work in communities and classrooms.* Cambridge, UK: Cambridge University Press

Holdaway, D (1979) *The foundations of literacy.* London: Ashton Scholastic

Hood, W (1994) 'Did they know he had slaves when they elected him?' Young children can ask powerful questions. In S. Steffey and W. Hood (Eds.) *If this is social studies, why isn't it boring?* York, ME: Stenhouse

Hoodless, P (Ed.) (1998) *History and English in the primary school: Exploiting the links.* London: Routledge

Huey, E (1908, 1972 reprint) *The Psychology and Pedagogy of Reading.* Cambridge, Mass: MIT Press

International Reading Association and National Association for the Education of Young Children (1998) *Learning to read and write: Developmentally Appropriate practices for young children.* Newark, DE: International Reading Association; Washington, DC: National Association for the Education of Young Children

Johnson, P (1995) *Children making books.* Reading, Berkshire, UK: University of Reading, Reading and Language Information Centre

Johnson, T. and Louis, D (1985) *Literacy through literature.* Melbourne, Australia: Thomas Nelson

Jones, R (1996) *Emerging patterns of literacy: A multidisciplinary perspective.* London: Routledge.

Kane, S (1999) Teaching decoding strategies without destroying story. *The Reading Teacher,* 52 p770-772

Karchmer, R (2000) Using the Internet and children's literature to support interdisciplinary instruction. *The Reading Teacher,* 54 p100-104

Kirby, P (1995) *Successful storysharing for parents and teachers.* Widnes, UK: United Kingdom Reading Association

Laminack, L (1991) *Learning with Zachary.* Richmond Hill, ON: Scholastic

Lane, H (2008) 'Let me tell you a story...' *The Guardian:* Family p4. 15.03.08

Lane, H. and Wright, T (2007) Maximizing the effectiveness of reading aloud. *The Reading Teacher,* 60 p668-675

Langer, J.A (1995) *Envisioning literature: Literary understanding and literature instruction.* New York: Teachers College Press

Marriott, S (1995) *Read on: Using fiction in the primary school.* London: Paul Chapman

Martens, P (1996) *I already know how to read: A child's view of literacy.* Portsmouth, NH: Heinemann

REFERENCES

McCarrier, A, Pinnell, G. and Fountas, I (1999) *Interactive writing: How language and literacy come together, K-2.* Portsmouth, NH: Heinemann

McGee, L (1995) Talking about books with young children. In N.L. Roser and M.G. Martinez (Eds.), *Book talk and beyond: Children and teachers respond to literature.* Newark, DE: International Reading Association

McGee, L. and Schickedanz, J (2007) 'Repeated interactive read-alouds in preschool and kindergarten', *The Reading Teacher* 60(8) p742-751

Meek, M (1988) *How texts teach what readers learn.* Stroud, UK: Thimble Press

Meek, M (1990) What do we know about reading that helps us to teach? In R. Carter (Ed.), *Knowledge about language and the curriculum.* London: Hodder and Stoughton

Money, T. (1987) Early literacy. In G. Blenkin and A. Kelly (Eds.), *Early childhood education: A developmental curriculum.* London: Paul Chapman

Mooney, M (1990) *Reading to, with, and by children.* Katonah, NY: Richard C. Owen

Morado, C *et al* (1999) Miniperformances, many stars! Playing with stories. *The Reading Teacher,* 53 p116-123

Morrow, L.M (1988) Young children's responses to one-to-one story readings in school settings. *Reading Research Quarterly,* 23 p89-107

Morrow, L.M (1989) Designing the classroom to promote literacy development. In D.S. Strickland and L.M. Morrow (Eds.), *Emerging literacy: Young children learn to read and write.* Newark, DE: International Reading Association

Morrow, L.M (1992) The impact of a literature-based program on literacy achievement, use of literature, and attitudes of children from minority backgrounds. *Reading Research Quarterly,* 27 p250-275

Moustafa, M (1997) *Beyond traditional phonics: Research discoveries and reading instruction.* Portsmouth, NH: Heinemann

Neuman, S (1998) How can we enable all children to achieve? In S.B. Neuman and K.A. Roskos (Eds.), *Children achieving: Best practices in early literacy.* Newark, DE: International Reading Association

Nicholson, D (2006) Putting literature at the heart of the literacy curriculum. *Literacy,* 40 (1) p11-21

Nutbrown, C (1994) *Threads of thinking: Young children learning and the role of early education.* London: Paul Chapman

Opie, I. and Opie, P (1959) *The lore and language of school children.* Oxford, UK: Oxford University Press

Opitz, M.F (2000) *Rhymes and reasons: Literature and language play for phonological awareness.* Portsmouth, NH: Heinemann

Pahl, K (1999) *Transformations: Children's meaning making in a nursery.* Stoke-on Trent, UK: Trentham Books

Parkes, B (2000) *Read It Again! Revisiting Shared Reading.* Portland, Maine: Stenhouse

Phillips, G. and McNaughton, S (1990) The practice of storybook reading to pre-schoolers in mainstream New Zealand families. *Reading Research Quarterly,* 25 p196-212

Phinn, G (2000) *Young readers and their books: Suggestions and strategies for using texts in the literacy hour.* London: David Fulton

Powell, D. and Hornsby, D (1998) Learning phonics while sharing and respond-ing to literature. In C. Weaver (Ed.), *Practicing what we know: Informed reading instruction.* Urbana, IL: National Council of Teachers of English

Rhodes, L (1981) I can read! Predictable books as resources for reading and writing instruction. *The Reading Teacher,* 34 p511-518

Rodgers, Y, Hawthorne, S and Wheeler, R (2007) Teaching Economics through Children's Literature in the Primary Grades. *The Reading Teacher,* 61(1) p46-55

Rose, J (2006) *Independent Review of the teaching of early reading, Final Report.* London: Department for Education and Skills

Rosen, M at MichaelRosen.co.uk (as accessed October 2008)

Rosenblatt, L.M (1978) *The reader, the text, the poem.* Cambridge, MA: Harvard University Press

Roser, N.L. and Martinez, M.G (Eds) (1995) *Book talk and beyond: Children and teachers respond to literature.* Newark, DE: International Reading Association

Routman, R (1991) *Invitations: Changing as teachers and learners K-12.* Ports-mouth, NH: Heinemann

Schickedanz, J.A (1990) *Adam's righting revolutions.* Portsmouth, NH: Heine-mann

Shatzer, J (2008) Picture Book Power: Connecting Children's Literature and Mathematics. *The Reading Teacher,* 61(8) p649-653

Short, K (1999) The search for 'balance' in literacy instruction. *English in Educa-tion,* 33(3) p43-53

Slaughter, J.P (1993) *Beyond storybooks: Young children and shared book experience.* Newark, DE: International Reading Association

Sloan, G.D (1991) *The child as critic: Teaching literature in elementary and middle schools* (3rd ed.). New York: Teachers College Press

Smith, J. and Elley, W (1994) *Learning to read in New Zealand.* Katonah, NY: Richard C. Owen

REFERENCES

Spreadbury, J (1994) *Read me a story: Parents, teachers and children as partners in literacy learning.* Carlton, Victoria, Australia: Australian Reading Association

Strickland, D.S (1998) *Teaching phonics today: A primer for educators.* Newark, DE: International Reading Association

Strickland, D.S. and Cullinan, B.E (1990) Afterword. In M.J. Adams, *Beginning to read: Thinking and learning about print.* Cambridge, MA: MIT Press

Strickland, D.S. and Morrow, L.M (1989) Interactive experiences with storybook reading. *The Reading Teacher,* 42 p322-323

Taylor, D., and Strickland, D.S (1986) *Family storybook reading.* New York: Scholastic

Teale, W (1984) Reading to young children: Its significance for literacy development. In H. Goelman, A. Oberg and F. Smith (Eds.), *Awakening to literacy.* London: Heinemann

Teale, W. and Sulzby, E (1989) Emergent literacy: New perspectives. In D.S. Strickland and L.M. Morrow (Eds.), *Emerging literacy: Young children learn to read and write.* Newark, DE: International Reading Association

Tizard, B. and Hughes, M (1984) *Young children learning: Talking and thinking at home and at school.* London: Fontana

Trelease, J (1995) *The read-aloud handbook* (4th ed.) New York: Penguin.

Wade, B. (Ed.). (1990). *Reading for real.* Buckingham, UK: Open University Press

Wade, B. and Moore, M (2000) *Baby Power.* Handforth, Cheshire: Egmont World Ltd

Watson, V (1993) Multi-layered texts and multi-layered readers. *Cambridge Journal of Education,* 23(1) p15-24

Weinberger, J., Hannon, P. and Nutbrown, C (1990) *Ways of working with parents to promote literacy development.* Sheffield, UK: University of Sheffield Division of Education

Wells, G (1986) *The meaning makers: Children learning language and using language to learn.* London: Hodder and Stoughton

White, D (1984 1st published 1954) *Books before five.* Portsmouth, NH: Heinemann.

Whitehead, M (1987) Narrative, stories and the world of literature. In G.Blenkin and A. Kelly (Eds), *Early childhood education: A developmental curriculum.* London: Paul Chapman

Whitehead, M (2002) Dylan's routes to literacy: The first three years with picture books. *Journal of Early Childhood Literacy.* 2 (3), p269-289

Wolf, M (2008) *Proust and the Squid: The story and science of the reading brain.* Cambridge: Icon Books.

Zambo, D (2007) Using picture books to provide archetypes to young boys: Extending the ideas of William Brozo. *The Reading Teacher* 61(2). p124-131

Children's books

Ahlberg, J. and Ahlberg, A (1978) *Each peach pear plum*. Harlow, UK: Oliver and Boyd

Alborough, J (2001) *Fix-It Duck*. London: Harper Collins

Amery, H (1989) *Barn on fire*. London: Usborne

Attwood, M (1995) *Princess Prunella and the Purple Peanut*. New York: Workman Publishing

Base, G (1986) *Animalia*. New York: Harry Abrams

Burton, V (1977) *Mike Mulligan and his steam shovel*. Harmondsworth, UK: Puffin Books

Butterfield, M (1995) *Zoo animals*. Loughborough, UK: Ladybird

Carle, E (1969) *The Very Hungry Caterpillar*. New York: Philomel Books

Carle, E (1990) *Pancakes, pancakes*. New York: Simon and Schuster

Carle, E (1991) *Do you want to be my friend?* Boston: Houghton Mifflin

Cronin, D (2002) *Giggle, Giggle, Quack*. London: Simon and Schuster

Dalgleish, J (1990) *The Snail and the Cherry Tree*. Cambridge: Cambridge University Press

Dodd, L (1983) *Hairy Maclary from Donaldson's Dairy*. Harmondsworth, UK: Puffin Books

Dodd, L (1985a) *Hairy Maclary scattercat*. Harmondsworth, UK: Puffin Books

Dodd, L (1985b) *Hairy Maclary's rumpus at the vet*. Harmondsworth, UK: Puffin Books

Dodd, L (1993) *Slinky Malinki, open the door*. Harmondsworth, UK: Puffin Books

Dodd, L (1995) *Sniff-snuff-snap!* Harmondsworth, UK: Puffin Books

Donaldson, J (1999) *The Gruffalo*. London: Macmillan

Donaldson, J (2003) *The Snail and the Whale*. London: Macmillan

Dunbar, J (1991) *Four fierce kittens.* London: Orchard Books

Fox, M (1983) *Possum magic.* New York: Harcourt Brace

Fox, M (1988) *Koala Lou.* New York: Harcourt Brace

Fox, M (1995) *Wombat Divine.* Sydney, Australia: Scholastic Australia Group

Hutchins, P (1972) *Good-night owl.* London: The Bodley Head

Hutchins, P (1987) *Rosie's walk.* New York: Scholastic

Kasza, K (1996) *The wolf's chicken stew.* New York: Putnam and Grosset

Lacome, J (1993) *Walking through the jungle.* London: Walker Books

Lenski, L (1946) *The little train.* Oxford, UK: Oxford University Press

Mayo, M (2002) '*Emergency!*' London: Orchard Books

Morpurgo, M (1999) *Kensuke's Kingdom.* London: Egmont

Oxenbury, H (1993) *It's my birthday.* London: Walker Books

Radcliffe, T (1997) *Cimru the seal.* Harmondsworth, UK: Puffin Books

Seuss, Dr (1960) *Green eggs and ham.* New York: Random House

Seuss, Dr (1963) *Hop on Pop.* New York: Random House

Waddell, M (1988) *Can't you sleep, little bear?* London: Walker Books

Waddell, M (1991) *Let's go home, little bear.* Cambridge, MA: Candlewick Press

Wadsworth, G (1999) *One tiger growls.* Watertown, MA: Charlesbridge

Walsh, J (1997) *When I was little like you.* Harmondsworth, UK: Puffin Books

Wilhelm, H (1985) *I'll always love you.* London: Hodder

Index